HIDDEN HISTORY *of* HAMILTON COUNTY INDIANA

David Heighway

THE History PRESS

Published by The History Press
Charleston, SC
www.historypress.com

First published 2021

Manufactured in the United States

ISBN 9781467150170

Library of Congress Control Number: 2021938360

To my family, for their love and support.

Contents

Contents

Acknowledgements

There are many people that I would like to thank who have helped on this book in various ways: the staff at the Hamilton East Public Library for their resources and patience while I worked on this, particularly Molly Mrozowski and Edra Waterman; the members of the Hamilton County Historical Society for their contributions, particularly Jessica Petty; Mike Corbett, editor and publisher of the *Hamilton County Business Magazine*; Bryan Glover for his help with topics of diversity; and my editor, John Rodrigue, for his guidance on the project. I would most like to thank my sister Anne and my brother Rob for their support and encouragement.

Introduction

Hamilton County, Indiana, is a pleasant, prosperous suburban area north of Indianapolis. However, like any community, there are layers of history that get overlooked or forgotten. This book will examine some of the elements of those layers.

This is a collection of stories that I have been creating over the years for the Hamilton East Public Library blog, the *Hamilton County Business Magazine* and other venues. Ever since I first wrote about the Great Squirrel Stampede in 2001, I've found that stories about oddball facts and little-known incidents have been my most popular stuff. After some examination, here's a theory that may explain why.

The present population of Hamilton County is mostly newer residents. During the first explosive growth of suburbia in the 1950s and 1960s, some communities lost their identity. Suburban sprawl made them lose focus on the heart of the community—usually the downtown area—and they lost some of their physical presence.

Now, there is a countywide emphasis on efforts to re-create the community centers. This requires the community to reestablish an identity. Residents' contacts aren't based on deep roots, so the usual collection of old county names is pretty meaningless. Instead, they have to find something that makes them unique, something peculiar or offbeat.

For example, if you were a resident of the county and were told that Levi P. Fodrea held the office of Hamilton County recorder for many years and was a highly respected citizen around the turn of the century, would you think that it mattered?

But suppose you were told that his son William was co-owner and chief engineer of the only car company in Hamilton County (see the Beetle Flyer story), but before that, he was the main suspect in a murder trial in which he was accused of killing a romantic rival. He was saved by two witnesses: a prostitute nicknamed Crazy Mick, who testified against him (but was considered unbelievable), and his sister Leota, who spoke for him. She was a young, beautiful and respected teacher whose tearful testimony moved the jury to acquit him. She was also a talented actress who rescued a locally written production from failure just by her performance (see the John Wise story). She might have done more but died at a tragically young age of pneumonia, just after she became engaged.

NOW we have a story.

This book will also explore the diversity of the area and look at the lives of people who have been left out of the written record before now. They made many contributions to the community that should be recognized. Their stories provide a unique texture to life in this county.

All in all, there is much more to the people of this area than has been written in the standard county histories. The stories in this book should give us some insight into their lives and show that they were people like us who were dealing with many issues. I hope that these strange stories might make them a little less strange.

Part I

OPENING THE COUNTY

Early Trails and Routes

The flow of people into the area now known as Hamilton County was affected by two ancient trails that were probably created by animal migration patterns. This was how a pathway was kept open in the dense forest. While elk would have been the most likely animal to have caused this, early pioneers contended that the path was created by buffalo. However, no remains of buffalo have been found in the county.

One trail was a north–south river-based route. It possibly started at Falls of the Ohio, went through present-day Clark County and then Scott, Jackson and Bartholomew Counties. It crossed the east fork of the White River at present-day Columbus. It met the west fork of the White River in Johnson County and followed it through Marion and Hamilton Counties. The trail crossed White River at a ford on the north side of Strawtown at Madison Street. It continued north to the meeting of three rivers now known as Fort Wayne. The route of the trail impacted the later routes of Allisonville Road, Highway 37 and Interstate 69.

The other trail, which went from southeast to northwest, probably started on the Ohio River near present-day Cincinnati. It went up through the Whitewater Valley and then through Henry County and Madison County. It followed White River to Strawtown along present Strawtown Avenue and crossed the river at a ford west of the present town. The trail then headed northwest, where towns like Cicero, Boxley, Kirkland, Frankfort and Lafayette would appear in the future. Something that supports the

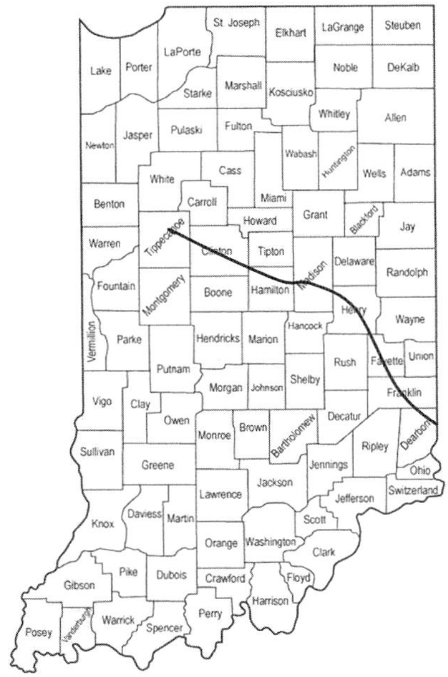

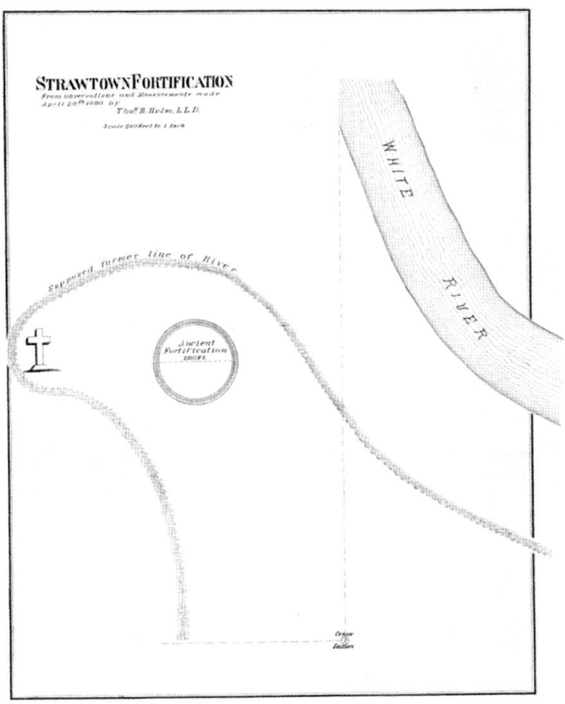

Above, left: Route of the Fort Wayne trail. *Author drawing.*

Above, right: Route of the Lafayette Trace. *Author drawing.*

Left: Map of the prehistoric settlement at Strawtown. *Drawing from Helm's* History of Hamilton County, *1880.*

idea of a migration route is that the Wea and Wildcat prairies on the Wabash River are good grazing ground. The trail was eventually called the Lafayette Trace.

The first humans appeared around 10,000 BCE. These were Paleoindians passing through as they hunted game and naturally followed the trails. Remnants of their hunting camps have been found along the river. Between 8,000 BCE and 1,500 BCE, the people called Archaic by archaeologists left evidence of some settlements. Real occupation started around AD 1000 and reached its height between AD 1200 and 1450 with a palisaded village at Strawtown. The archaeological remains are similar to those at Anderson and New Castle, which were along the Trace. There is evidence of trade with distant societies.[1]

In the 1600s, the tribe known as the Miami began to appear and became dominant in the area, along with tribes like the Potawatomi and Wea.

Newcomers

Nonnative fur traders may have begun appearing in the area by 1717. That was when the French trading post at Ouiatenon on the Wabash River was established, and the Trace would have been a useful route to get there. Despite this, the area seems to have had little involvement in the disagreements between the French and the British over control of the land north of the Ohio River. The area became part of the Northwest Territory when it was established in 1787 after the American Revolution

The trails were possibly used as a route during the series of battles known as the Northwest Indian War. The explorer William Clark (later of Lewis and Clark) was part of a military expedition in 1791 that may have used the trails to get from the Wabash River to the Falls of the Ohio.[2] With the Treaty of Greenville in 1795 ending the war, the Lenape (Delaware) Indians and their allied tribe, the Nanticoke, arrived from the east and established towns along the river. Chief Anderson—whose Lenape name was Kikthawenund—eventually became leader. Andersontown was the main community, but Strawtown was significant. In 1800, the Indiana Territory was created with William Henry Harrison as governor.

In 1802, the man who is recognized as the first permanent settler came to the area. William Conner (1777–1855) arrived to establish a trading post. However, he was not the only one. The Brouilette family from Vincennes had established a post at Strawtown, leaving Conner to establish his post farther downriver at a site later called Jordan's Ford. Conner then took a Delaware

William Conner. *Portrait from* Indiana and Indianans *by Jacob Piatt Dunn, 1919.*

woman as his wife. Her name was Mekinges, and as a daughter of Chief Anderson, she was well connected. (Importantly, the Delaware tribe is matrilineal, which means that the mother determines the clan of the child. Still, her connections to the chief would have been useful.)

The Lafayette Trace may have been used by Tecumseh to travel between Prophetstown and Andersontown as he tried to get Chief Anderson to join his confederacy. One source says that the Delaware requested aid and protection from William Henry Harrison during Tecumseh's 1811 uprising, to which Harrison responded by stationing cavalry at Strawtown.[3] However, during the War of 1812, the Delaware abandoned Strawtown and retreated to Ohio.

The trails through this area were used for raids by both Native Americans and Indiana militia during the war.

On June 11, 1813, Colonel Joseph Bartholomew of the Indiana Rangers set out from Fort Vallonia up the west fork of the White River with 137 men to deal with the rising number of hostile attacks by Miami and Potawatomi Indians. They saw several burned villages along the river, and on June 17, 9 of the soldiers clashed with 2 Indians near Strawtown. One of the Indians was killed, and 1 of the soldiers was fatally wounded.[4]

On July 1, 1813, Colonel William Russell, of the Seventh U.S. Infantry, assembled a force of 573 men (which included future president Zachary Taylor) to do a "scout" for hostile Indians. The route went from Vallonia to the villages on White River to the Mississinewa villages and then to the Wabash River and down through Prophetstown to Fort Harrison and ended at Vincennes, a trip that covered about five hundred miles. No Indians were seen, and all of the villages were found to be deserted.[5]

William Conner left his trading post and served with the army at several battles, including the Battle of the Thames, where Tecumseh was killed. The Delaware Indians returned to this area in 1815 after the war was over.

The Native American presence in the Hamilton County area was ended by the Treaty of St. Mary's in 1818. The main treaty was with the Miamis, the preeminent tribe in Indiana. This treaty was signed at St. Mary's, Ohio, on October 6, 1818. However, the area that would become Hamilton

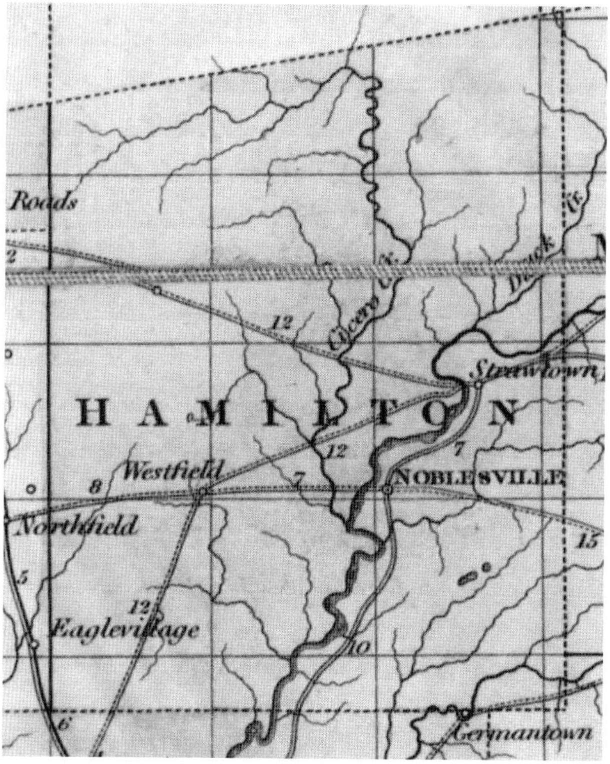

Map of Hamilton County showing early trails, roads and settlements. Detail from *The American Atlas* by Burr and Arrowsmith, 1839. *Library of Congress.*

County was occupied primarily by the Delaware or Lenape Indians. A separate treaty made with the Delawares was signed on October 3 by Chief Anderson and other Delaware leaders, most of whom lived in what today is Madison County.[6]

The area became known as the Delaware New Purchase. This larger area was soon broken up into sections called Wabash County, which covered the Wabash River drainage area, and Delaware County, which covered the White River drainage area. This put the future Hamilton County in Delaware County, which is how people from the area were listed in the 1820 national census. The Delaware New Purchase eventually became about thirty-five different counties. This would include Hamilton County, but first there had to be enough residents to legally incorporate it.[7]

Who Was Pete Smith?

The Mystery of Noblesville's First Settler

A very important story in the founding of the county was that of Pete Smith and his contribution. Smith was a Black man and was the first non-Indian to live in the Noblesville area. It was through his efforts that the first white settlers were able to survive. He left no records himself, and the information we do have is based on reminiscences written down sixty years or more after the fact. Nevertheless, his story illustrates some important facts about the early settlement of the area and should be told if we are to understand how this community was created.

What we know of his life begins in the year 1819. The Treaty of St. Mary's, signed in 1818 between the Delaware Indians and the federal government, had opened the land that would become Hamilton County for settlement. There were already some traders living here, including William Conner, who had arrived in 1802. The traders then left for new territory or, like Conner, began purchasing government land to resell to the new settlers. In April 1819, a group of these settlers set out from southern Indiana to stake a claim in the new territory. This was the Finch and Shirts families, along with some others. Originally from New York and New England, they came to this area via the Lafayette Trace, an ancient Indian trail that came up from the Whitewater Valley, through what would become New Castle and Anderson and crossed the White River at Strawtown. The group turned south at White River and followed another Indian trail to a large bend in the river where there had once been a Delaware village. The cleared flat land in this bend was perfect to begin farming and was called Horseshoe Prairie.

The group set up tents to live in until they could get cabins built and almost immediately suffered a disaster. A limb broke off a tree, falling on one of the tents and shattering most of the dinnerware that the group had brought with them. It was an inauspicious beginning. In order to be able to purchase the land, the settlers would have to make improvements—build houses, clear the land and begin growing crops. They persevered and began to create a community in the wilderness.

It was at this time that Pete Smith appeared. There were some Delaware Indian families who had not left the area yet. Smith was living with one of the families and simply showed up at the settlement one day. Described later as "fine looking" and "intelligent," Smith attracted attention, as no one expected to see a Black man in this area. He told them nothing about where he had come from or why he was there but instead offered to help them. At first, the settlers weren't quite sure what to make of this man, but he soon proved his worth.

One day in June, after a day of working in the fields, Mrs. Finch left her muddy shoes outside her cabin. When she awoke the next morning, they were gone. This was of serious concern, as the nearest place to buy shoes was Connersville, sixty miles away. The Delaware Indians remaining in the area were the first suspects, and some of the settlers wanted to confront them. However, Pete Smith intervened and asked the settlers not to take any action. He told Mrs. Finch to be patient and her shoes would come back to her. The settlers decided to take him at his word. They finished up the day and went to bed.

Evidently, Smith did something that night, because the next morning when Mrs. Finch awoke, her shoes were outside the cabin door. Smith refused to say what he had done or where the shoes had come from, but as one settler later said, "He was the hero of the little colony." It was very fortunate he took the action he did. A few years later, a confrontation between the Indians and another group of settlers would end in horrific tragedy and be known as the Massacre on Fall Creek.

Smith became a trusted friend of the settlers and proved his worth again and again. That summer, the settlement was ravaged by malaria. George Shirts's wife was the first to die, and Smith helped Shirts raise his corn. Others would die, and many would be too sick to work. Smith continued to help, but food began to run short. The settlement survived by buying corn from William Conner. He charged them one dollar a bushel, roughly the price of a full deerskin. The sickness eventually subsided, probably at the beginning of the cold weather when the mosquitoes that caused it disappeared.

In 1820, Smith was working for William Conner, raising a field of corn and doing some trapping on his own. That was a busy year for Conner. In May, at a meeting at his house, the site for the capital of the state was chosen and would be named Indianapolis. In August, most of the Delaware Indians left Indiana. Conner's wife, a Delaware named Mekinges, left with her people, taking with her the six children she and Conner had produced. Conner stayed behind and, three months later, married Elizabeth Chapman, a relative of one of the early settlers and the only available white woman in the area. In all probability, Smith was helping the settlers and working for Conner because he planned to stay with the settlement. He did not leave with the Indians when he had the opportunity. He may have been planning to establish his own home and farm. Sadly, this was not to happen.

By 1821, land buyers were coming in from all over to speculate in these newly available western lands. That year, a man came up from Kentucky to purchase land to resell. According to later accounts, he saw Smith, returned to Kentucky and soon reappeared in this area with a group of men and some sort of papers saying that Pete Smith was his runaway slave. Smith said that he didn't even know the man. The settlers confronted the man from Kentucky, and as one of them later said, "It created intense excitement and there might have been a lynching of the slave-hunters." However, at this point, William Conner happened on the scene.

Conner was a man of influence in the county, and the settlers appealed to him to intervene to free Smith. He would disappoint them. He examined the Kentuckian's papers and announced that they were legally correct. He then said that if the settlers attempted to stop the Kentuckian, they would be guilty of breaking the law. Without this support, the settlers could do nothing. The Kentuckian took Smith away, and he was never heard from again.

Conner sold the corn that Smith had raised for him. The settlers themselves would soon experience the difference between what was legal and what was right. They had been improving their lands so that they could buy them from the government. In 1822, William Conner's brother John went to the land office in Connersville and bought their land out from beneath them. He would give them until the harvest to leave the land. Most of them moved to Wayne Township. In 1823, William Conner and Josiah Polk established the town of Noblesville just north of the old settlement at Horseshoe Prairie.

Was Pete Smith a runaway slave? We will never know the answer, but some guesses can be made. Since Smith made no attempt to leave after the first appearance of the Kentuckian, it would seem unlikely that he knew the man. Then what was happening? Sadly, there are many instances in early

American history of slave hunters kidnapping free Blacks out of the free states. A man like Pete Smith would have been worth a lot of money in the slave markets. The documents used to capture slaves were often rudimentary descriptions that might have applied to anyone. It was possible that Smith was actually just a trapper and trader. His easy familiarity with the area suggests that he had been there for some time. There were some examples of Black people who made their living trading with the Indians, the most famous being Jean Baptiste DuSable, the first settler of Chicago.

It is encouraging that the settlers tried to stand up for Smith. When they talked about him in their later reminiscences, they would describe him as having a "good disposition," "a kind heart," "ready to assist" and "thoroughly honest." One hopes that Smith did not end his days on a Kentucky plantation. There may be a clue uncovered by Indiana Freedom Trails, a group dedicated to the study of the Underground Railroad in Indiana. They have found a story about a slave named Peter escaping from a Kentucky slave owner in August 1821. He was nearly recaptured in 1825 in Wayne County, Indiana. However, a local group of people broke into the jail where he was held and freed him. He escaped and was not heard from again. To live out his days in freedom would be a much more fitting life for Pete Smith, Noblesville's first settler.[8]

The Great Squirrel Stampede

For being such a small and innocuous animal, the common squirrel has aroused a great deal of animosity through the years. Its cleverness and persistence in getting food has naturally antagonized anyone who might want to keep some food for their own use. Any person who has ever owned a bird feeder would understand the pioneers' frustration at being unable to keep squirrels out of their gardens and cornfields. However, in the early part of the nineteenth century, it was not feeder acrobatics that threatened the humans' food stores. It was sheer numbers of animals. While almost forgotten now, the enormous waves of squirrels that swept across the United States in the 1800s were as much concern at that time as locusts or disease.

In 1901, Noblesville lawyer Augustus F. Shirts (1824–1905) wrote a book called *A History of the Formation, Settlement, and Development of Hamilton County, Indiana, from the Year 1818 to the Close of the Civil War*. It was devoted largely to stories about pioneer life in this county. One story went as follows:

> *In the year of 1826 the great emigration of squirrels occurred. The squirrels passed through this county from west to east. The number could not be estimated. The time occupied in passing was about two weeks. They destroyed all the corn in the fields they passed over. They could not be turned in their course, but went straight on in the route taken. When they came to White River they entered the water at once and swam across. Hundreds of them were shot. Others were killed with clubs and stones. It was never known from whence they came or where they went.*[9]

Augustus Finch Shirts. *Portrait from Shirts's* Primitive History of Hamilton County, *1901.*

At one time, this was dismissed as folklore, but since Shirts's parents were among the first settlers of Hamilton County, he probably heard it firsthand. Allowing for some discrepancy in dates, there are plenty of eyewitnesses to this flood of rodents, as well as modern scientific justification.

One eyewitness was Calvin Fletcher (1798–1866), an Indianapolis lawyer, banker and civic leader who kept a diary throughout most of his adult life.[10] Combined with his letters, this is an excellent resource for early central Indiana history. In a letter to his brother dated February 23, 1823, he states:

> *The corn this year was literally destroyed, unless in the prairies, by grey and black squirrel. Sir, there was by one man killed round one cornfield 248 in 3 days about 4 miles of this place. Many people lost whole cornfields—12* [squirrels] *were supposed to destroy as much corn as one hog. They eat only the heart or pit of the kernel. The squirrel appeared to be emigrating towards the S.W. instead of the E. as he has always done heretofore. The reason for his emigration this year was this—our woods or wilderness, it scarcely ever fails to produce a sufficient quantity of mast to support such vermin but this year they entirely fail'd—the word mast is used by the people here for the fruit and nuts that grow on forrest trees.*

Another firsthand observer was Oliver Johnson (1821–1907). He lived in a cabin that his parents built in 1822 at what is now Thirty-Eighth Street and Fall Creek Boulevard in Indianapolis. In his later years, he reminisced about his early life to his grandson Howard, who wrote down his tales under the title *A Home in the Woods*.[11] He told many stories about hunting, including the following:

> *Squirrels were always so plentiful that we saved only the choice parts: the hams and the back. We always shot a squirrel in the head so that the bullet wouldn't spoil those parts. In the fall we nearly always had a spell of travelin' squirrels. We supposed that the mast and nuts that they fed on was scarce in some sections and caused them to move on to other places where they could find something to eat.*
>
> *One fall there was so many passin' through they became a pest, makin' raids on the corn fields. They come by the thousands for several days. They was so starved and footsore from travelin' that they wasn't fit to eat. Pap said something had to be done, so he put Uncle Milt and me to patrollin' the corn field with our rifles. At night we would mould enough bullets to keep us shootin' all the next day. The squirrels was so hungry they didn't scare very much, but the crack of the rifles helped to keep them up in the trees.*
>
> *One day I counted eighteen dead squirrels I shot from a tree without changin' position or missin' a shot. We left so many dead ones on the ground that they actually attracted the buzzards. We saved most of our corn that fall, but some neighbors who didn't patrol their fields had their corn eat up so bad it didn't pay to gather it.*

John James Audubon (1785–1851) is considered one of the greatest naturalists America ever produced. He witnessed several great squirrel emigrations, including ones that crossed the Ohio and Hudson Rivers. He was impressed with their ability to swim or to grab floating objects in their effort to reach the other shore, even though many drowned. In his 1846 book *Viviparous Quadrupeds of North America*, he said, "The farmers in the Western wilds regard them with sensations which may be compared to the anxious apprehensions of the Eastern nations at the sight of the devouring locust." However, he made an error about the squirrels when he declared the migratory squirrel to be a separate species. It was actually the common gray squirrel (*Sciurus carolinensis*) that Audubon saw swimming the rivers.

According to some early Indiana histories, there were two great squirrel emigrations in central Indiana, in 1822 and 1845. There were other smaller

John James Audubon painting of "migratory squirrel." *From* Viviparous Quadrupeds of North America, *1849.*

movements in various parts of the state in the early nineteenth century.[12] Nationally, there were several multistate emigrations, including an enormous one in 1842 that swept from Iowa to Wisconsin. Rough descriptions suggest it was 130 miles wide by 150 miles long. One person viewing an area of road only a few yards wide guessed he could see 1,400 animals. A modern scientist estimated that the emigration contained half a billion squirrels.[13]

Naturalists contend that the regular migration of small groups of squirrels is a form of population dispersal. The movements are referred to as "emigrations" because, unlike a migration, the animals do not return to their home country. Naturalists are not certain what would cause the larger movements, although most think environmental pressure seems to be an obvious answer. The large emigrations usually occurred when a time of plentiful food was followed by a time of scarce food.[14]

Presumably, these emigrations had gone on for centuries. Prior to settlement by Europeans, the area east of the Mississippi River was covered in an almost continuous forest. Squirrels could swarm from the Atlantic coast to the Mississippi and never have to touch the ground. Although the Native Americans were probably aware of these movements (which would have been very useful for hunting), their reaction was not recorded. The emigrations first began to be noticed when the settlers moved in and began clearing the forest. A mob of starving squirrels that suddenly came upon a cornfield would cause a very obvious reaction. However, as more forests disappeared, the squirrels' habitats and mobility were greatly altered.

Reports of large emigrations have become almost nonexistent in the United States today. One was reported in the eastern United States in 1968, and another occurred near Lake Michigan in 1985. Estimates of numbers of animals are based on the amount of roadkill left behind. The feeling among scientists is that the environment has been changed so profoundly that the squirrels' behavior has changed in response. And while is it unlikely that they will ever be put on the endangered species list, the population of squirrels today is smaller than in the 1800s. With less pressure on the food supply, they have become more sedentary. In all probability, the sight of great herds of squirrels swarming through the trees and cornfields is now a thing of the past. So, the next time you throw a few curses at the furry-tailed thief in your bird feeder, be grateful for the fact that he hasn't brought several thousand of his friends with him.

ADVERTISING LAND

In studying old newspaper reports, it's important to not take the report at face value and to do some analysis. For example, look at the first description of Hamilton County in the media. This is from the July 2, 1823 edition of the *Indiana Intelligencer*, which was published in Charlestown, Clark County, Indiana. This is it reprinted in full, with all punctuation as it was in the original (and it's all one paragraph, so be prepared for a wall of text):

> *WEST FORK OF WHITE RIVER ABOVE INDIANAPOLIS*
> *This river might, with very little expense, be rendered navigable for 100 miles above this place, the greatest obstructions being the large rocks that lie scattered over the ripples, which are not seen when the water is high. It runs with a much more gentle current than is usual to find streams of the same size, except over the ripples, which are frequently several miles apart. The country through which the stream passes for the above distance, taking soil, timber, and all of the conveniences together, is not surpassed by any of the same extant in the western country. The land is all susceptible of cultivation, and is selling rapidly. Scattered along each side of the river, there are a great many small prairies, containing from 50 to 500 acres, the soil of which is remarkably rich. Several of these are already in a high state of cultivation; one particularly, containing about 200 acres all under fence, the property of Mr. ------- is covered with a luxuriant crop of wheat, rye, and corn. Adjoining to this is a piece of rising ground, on which the*

> *gentleman is building an elegant house of brick, and making other extensive and useful improvements suitable for a large farm from which he has a commanding view of all the land under fence, and can see very distinctly with the naked eye to the most distant part of his domains. A short distance above this is another of rather larger size, where there are extensive mill works erecting, which will be in operation later this fall. Not far above the latter place it is probable ~~the~~ seat of justice for Hamilton County will be located, as the county will be in complete organization during the present year. —Censor.*

This may be a form of what today is called "advertorial content," which means that it looks like an article but is actually meant to promote or sell something. The first sentence is a lie. Navigation for large boats on the west fork of the White River ends far downstream from Indianapolis. Flatboats might be used at certain times of the year.

While the description of the soil and prairies is true, the writer neglects to say that many of the prairies were former Delaware Indian villages and farms and had already been cleared. The Delaware Indians had left the area only a few years earlier.

The glowing description of the farm of "Mr. ------" (who is, of course, William Conner) would make one wonder if Conner himself had hired someone to write it. At this time, he and Josiah Polk were very busy buying up land and reselling it to incoming settlers.

The phase "A short distance above this is another…" is poorly worded but refers to the next big prairie to the north, which is Horseshoe Prairie, just south of Noblesville. The "extensive mill works" were built by William Conner's brother John and consisted of a single wooden mill with a couple of river rocks rigged for grinding. Incidentally, the mill was on property that John Conner had bought out from underneath the original settlers, who he then evicted.

Noblesville did not become the county seat until 1824, and the statement that the county government was still being organized in July 1823 was not a good sign. The state legislature had approved the incorporation of the county back in January.

So, it's a fun article, but it should be taken with a grain of salt. A little skepticism is always handy when following the news. Particularly nearly two hundred years after it's been published.

Pioneer Kids

Crossing the County in 1824

Recollections of the Early Settlement of the Wabash Valley by Sandford Cox was published in 1860 and gives a unique account of traveling through Hamilton County in the earliest time of settlement.

Sandford Cull Cox (also spelled "Sanford") was born on July 1, 1811, near Richmond in Wayne County, Indiana, and died on October 4, 1877, at Lafayette, Tippecanoe County, Indiana. In 1859, he wrote a series of articles in the *LaFayette Daily Courier* about the first settlers in the area, and the articles were later collected into the book. One of his sources was the journal of the "Black Creek School Master," who some say was actually Cox himself.[15]

This journal describes the author's family traveling by oxcart in October 1824 from Pendleton in Madison County to Thorntown in Boone County. They followed the Lafayette Trace—the early trail running from the Ohio River to the Wabash River that passed through Hamilton County. The route of the Trace can be seen on the 1866 map of the county.

While they were at Pendleton, they saw the men who were on trial for the famous Massacre on Fall Creek. On the first day of the journey, October 25, they got as far as Strawtown, which he referred to as "Abbott's Ford," and camped overnight. When they began the next morning and crossed White River, there was a cabin by the roadside. The driver of the oxcart pointed to the cabin and told them to take a good look, as it would be the last house they would see for forty miles.

At that time, the area was an immense forest, and getting lost was extremely easy. The family's sheep wandered off the trail into the forest, and in chasing them, the author got lost as well. He was terrified but was found after a few hours. The sheep were considered to be lost beyond hope, and the family left without them.

That night, there was a rainstorm with strong winds. It stopped before morning, but the temperature dropped and there was frost on the ground at sunrise. As they were preparing to leave their campsite, the author's younger brother became lost, and they were delayed a few hours until they found him.

At noon, they reached Cicero Creek and were fortunate to find half a deer carcass that some previous traveler had salted and roasted to leave for other people on the road. It was considered a kind gesture (although today, sanitation issues might be a concern). They then tried to increase their pace to be able to reach a spring that was the only water source between Cicero Creek and Thorntown. They were unable to reach it that day, and the author said that he suffered from thirst so intense that "I could not refrain from stooping down and drinking out of a horse track in the road, shutting my eyes lest I might see wigglers in the water."

After an uncomfortable night, they reached the water source the next morning. It was a spring called "Brown's Wonder," and there is a church by that name today just north of Lebanon. After meeting up with some old acquaintances who had been to the Wabash and were traveling back along the road, they continued on their way. They camped at another water source that night and reached Thorntown on the morning of October 29.

Today, a trip from Pendleton to Thorntown takes about an hour, depending on the route you choose.

Early Hazards of Teaching

The first schools dealt with many things that teachers would recognize today, including a lack of supplies and spotty attendance (by teachers as well as students). However, an aspect not usually thought of was dealing with wild animals, particularly a dangerous animal that was very real: wolves. In the early nineteenth century, they were common in this area.

In his 1911 book about the history of the Carmel area, *Reminiscences of the Long Ago*, Zina Warren writes:

> *One night the wolves were howling and they had forgotten to shut the hogs up, and my elder brothers went in the dark to shut them up. Another time they neglected to put the sheep in the fold, and in the morning "A field of the dead rushed red on their sight, and the lambs and sheep were scattered in the fight." A long pasture field was strewn with dead sheep from one end to the other.*[16]

Augustus Finch Shirts wrote in his 1901 book:

> *The wolves were very plentiful and were very bold and troublesome, frequently coming near to the buildings and picking up pigs and lambs and carrying them off. They sometimes attacked young calves, so that the pioneers, in addition to the vast amount of hard work to be done, were compelled to be on the watch for these and other wild beasts. The wolves were shot to death whenever and wherever found. They were also caught*

> *in traps. In fact, a regular fight was made against them with a view to their extermination.*[17]

Occasionally, the wolves fought back. The most well-known attack happened because of the first school in White River Township. It was near Strawtown on the farm of Michael French and was in session during the winters of 1822–23 and 1823–24. The teacher and near-victim of the attack was Dr. Amos Palmer. He was the first physician in Strawtown, county assessor in 1837 and county auditor in 1846.

According to A.F. Shirts:

> *Dr. Amos Palmer, while teaching school at Strawtown, made his home with John Finch, four miles southeast of Noblesville. His habit was to leave the vicinity of the school house on Friday evening and Finch's on Sunday evening. On one occasion, there being good moonlight, he left the Finches after nightfall. Palmer was making the trip on foot. The route was mainly through the woods. He followed a trace leading from the Finch place to Strawtown. This trace crossed Stony Creek near the north line of lands now owned by Charles Zeis. There were plenty of wolves and panthers in the woods and occasionally a bear, so Palmer secured a good stout stick before starting from Finch's. Soon after crossing Stony Creek he was suddenly attacked by a number of wolves. Although taken by surprise, he used his stick as best he could and succeeded in keeping them off of himself. He finally found a low limb upon a tree, which he believed he could reach by a vigorous leap. He made the effort and succeeded. He was for the time being safe, although the wolves made several attempts to reach him, but without success. How long he remained in this tree he could never tell. The welcome crack of the rifle and the barking of dogs gave him great comfort. The wolves on hearing the gun crack and the dogs bark left at once and Palmer was safe. To a party of hunters near by with their dogs Palmer owed his escape.*[18]

The Finch farm was near the present intersection of Highway 38 and Boden Road.

Shirts said that wolves could still be heard howling in Noblesville Township in 1830. However, the hunting took its toll. In 1859, there were only three wolf hides sold in Noblesville. Most naturalists think that wolves were gone from the state by 1908.

The First Map of the County

In the early nineteenth century, one of the duties of the U.S. Congress was to establish postal routes. That is particularly important for this area because it led to the first appearance in public media of the town of Noblesville.

It was shown on a map of the post roads of the United States published in 1825. The 1825 map is the first representation of Hamilton County that exists. The original survey had been done in 1821–22, which is why the county is covered in squares. The county government and the town of Noblesville had been established in January 1823 and are the only two legal entities on the map. There was some settlement around William Conner's homestead and around Strawtown, but they were not considered organized communities.

There wasn't much of Noblesville at that point in time. A noted Indiana businessman named Calvin Fletcher came through on May 20, 1824, on a trip from Indianapolis to Ludlow, Vermont, and wrote in his diary, "We went by way of Noblesvill [*sic*] which is laid off on the N. side of White R. in a very thickly timbered country—not a stick missing. We here took a little refreshment and proceeded on to Strawtown." The snarky comment about the lack of cleared land—"not a stick missing"—is pretty rich coming from someone living in Indianapolis, which had only been established in 1820.[19]

Although little existed of the town, the establishment of the postal route meant that it would be considered more of a destination. Promotion of the area was needed. The first known mention of the town in any newspaper

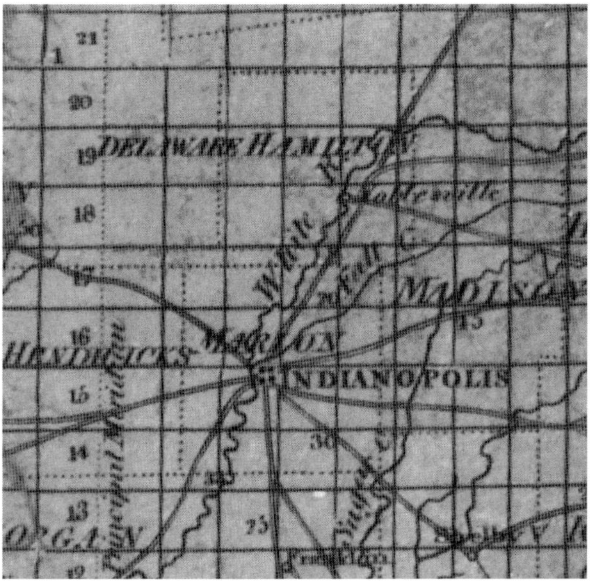

The first known map of Hamilton County. Detail from *Map of the United States* by Abraham Bradley, 1825. *Library of Congress.*

was when Josiah Polk, one of the founders of Noblesville, put land sales advertisements in the Richmond, Indiana newspaper in 1824.

The first known appearance of Noblesville in a newspaper outside Indiana was in the April 1, 1825 edition of the *American Watchman* and *Delaware Advertiser* (from Wilmington, Delaware) as part of a listing of national post roads established by Congress. The town was the stopping point between Winchester and Indianapolis. These post road announcements continued and expanded into the 1830s, when the state of Indiana began to do a lot more development of its own roads.

This Little Piggy Went to Market

Transportation of goods to market is a crucial link in any business. Today, the price of fuel has a huge impact on the price of groceries in the supermarket. However, the process now is still much simpler than it was 175 years ago. When Hamilton County was first settled, most farmers were concerned with feeding their own families. After a few years though, they began to produce a surplus and started looking for markets.

In his history of Hamilton County written in 1901, Augustus Finch Shirts described early agricultural economics. His family had moved to the county in 1819, and he had grown up here. He said that after the introduction of fanning mills into the county, farmers began to raise a surplus of wheat. However, there were no markets other than Cincinnati, Lawrenceburg or Lafayette. The farmers would load twenty bushels of wheat into a wagon and drive for four or five days to get to the market, where they would be paid around forty cents a bushel for the wheat and spend three days driving home.

It was even more labor intensive to get hogs to market. Livestock surpluses started appearing after 1835. Local merchants would buy the hogs in the autumn, collect them together and hire men to drive them to Cincinnati. In this case, "driving" meant walking the hogs all the way to Ohio with wagons used mostly just for supplies. Shirts described one drive that he participated in when he was a young boy:

> *We left Noblesville about the 3rd day of December, with ten hands and three teams. For two or three days we had fair weather and got along fairly well. It then began to rain and the roads soon became muddy. Some of the hogs traveled faster than others, so the hogs were divided into lots. The tired hogs would be placed in the wagons and hauled to the stopping place for the night. These tired hogs were lifted out of the mud and placed in the wagons by the hands in charge of the hindmost lot. After the rain set in these men would be at night wet to the skin. The men were kept on the road until dark and sometimes later. It frequently happened that after turning in at night the men were required to gather corn from the fields to feed the hogs that night, and the morning after. The hogs were usually fed about 4 o'clock in the morning and turned into the road at daylight. The process was continued from day to day until Cincinnati was reached, then the hands were turned loose with money enough to take them home. From twenty-one to twenty-two days were consumed in the trip. We wore the same suit of clothes all the time. At night we would dry them and the next morning rub the mud off and put them on. For my service I received 18 cents per day and board.*[20]

When the hogs reached Cincinnati, they would be sold for $1.50 to $1.75 per hundredweight. Cincinnati had become the nation's chief hog packing center by 1835, with the nickname of "Porkopolis."

The issues of transportation changed in 1851 with the completion of the railroad from Indianapolis to Noblesville. It would reach Peru in 1854. Hogs could now be put aboard railroad cars in Noblesville and shipped straight to Madison, where they would be transferred to boats headed for Cincinnati. Eventually there would also be the Monon Railroad, which went straight to Chicago. Not only was it cheaper and easier to ship livestock and produce, you also didn't have to wear the same suit of clothes for twenty-one days.

Thomas Murphy

An African American Pioneer

After Pete Smith, the second African American settler in the county was Thomas Murphy. Murphy was born in Virginia on June 8, 1808, and came to Hamilton County in the 1820s. While we have more information about him than we do about Smith, there is still not much, and some of that is questionable. Most of it comes from his obituary.[21]

The information about Murphy is obscure because he was primarily known as someone who accompanied George Boxley into Indiana. Boxley was an abolitionist who fled Virginia after being arrested for fomenting a slave rebellion. Murphy's obituary says he was brought to Ohio by another family (which is perhaps where he got the last name Murphy) and joined the Boxley family later. However, the obituary also says that Murphy got a job in Noblesville in 1823, while most sources say that Boxley settled in Hamilton County around 1827. Murphy is unmentioned in an anonymous document that claims to be a biography of George Boxley called *A Man with a Price on His Head*.[22]

Of the facts we do know: in the 1820 census, there were three African Americans living in the Delaware New Purchase created by the Treaty of St. Mary's. This encompassed thirty-one present counties in central Indiana, and it would be impossible to know where they lived. In the 1830 census, the counties had been divided up and Hamilton County had been created. There was one African American in the county: a male between the ages of ten and twenty-four living with the George Boxley family in Adams Township. This describes Murphy exactly.

The restored cabin of George Boxley in Sheridan, where Thomas Murphy lived in the early part of his life. *Author photo.*

Murphy did work in Noblesville at some point. Joseph Ross remembered working with him for Conner and Stephenson, later Conner and Cole, hauling and stacking furs in the store that was on the corner where Sunrise Café is today. They worked with furs from raccoons, foxes, muskrats, beavers, deer, wildcats, wolves and some otters, which were becoming scarce. The obituary said that Murphy eventually became head clerk.[23]

The obituary then says that around 1840 he moved to Strawtown, which was still an important stopping point on the Lafayette Trace. However, he hasn't been found in the 1840 census. The Eli Goin family were the only African Americans in White River Township at that time. Interestingly, Goin was also from Virginia. Murphy married Drusilla Goin on July 21, 1841 (his obituary says 1851), and his first son, Warren, was born in 1848.[24]

In 1846, Murphy moved to the town of Boxley, which was also along the Trace. While he was successful at first, this was probably not a good idea. A new road connecting Noblesville and Lafayette had been built farther south—it's now Highway 38—and was taking traffic from the Trace. The Adams Township 1850 census says that Murphy was a merchant and farmer with real estate valued at $3,000. There is some strange phrasing in his obituary at this point, but it sounds like he was cheated by a business partner and went bankrupt.

He moved to Tipton in 1856, built a house and started a grocery. This may have been when his first wife, Drusilla, died. The grocery burned in 1857, and he lost everything. He married his second wife, Jane Goin, on April 12, 1858. Between his two wives, he had nine children. He was running a grocery in 1860, according to the census. In 1870, he is listed as a farmer, and in 1880, he is listed as a laborer. He died on April 11, 1881, and is buried in Fairview Cemetery in Tipton. His house was torn down in 1895. Both Joseph Ross and the obituary said that Murphy was well known and apparently well liked in Tipton. It's somewhat surprising that there is very little information about him.[25]

The First Nature Preserve in Hamilton County

James Farley's Deer Park

With the growth of the county, the various municipal parks departments have moved quickly to try to preserve some natural scenic areas. Interestingly, an effort was made not long after the county was founded, when one of the first settlers of Delaware Township established a nature preserve of his own.

James Farley was born in Virginia in 1795 and came to Hamilton County sometime in the early 1830s. His first land purchase was in a section of Clay Township in 1835. However, he soon moved over to Delaware Township and did something very unique. Augustus Finch Shirts, in his 1901 history of the county, says, "In an early day, Mr. Farley laid off and set aside several acres of his land to be used for a park for deer. This park was surrounded by a high rail fence. Mr. Farley was proud of his deer park and maintained it for a long time."[26]

This was an odd thing to do in pioneer Indiana. Deer parks had existed in Europe since medieval times. They were a section of land used by the nobility for preserving and hunting deer. It would seem silly and pretentious here in the United States because at that time, deer were considered little better than pests. Still, land was cheap and there was plenty of it. If a person wanted to do something like this, he was free to do so.

It's not clear where the parkland actually was. The property owned by Farley was on the south side of where Keystone Avenue and 106th Street intersect today and went all the way south to 96th Street. Farley established a school at the corner of present-day LaSalle Road and 106th in 1837. In

1838, he established the Farley Cemetery, which can be seen today just southeast of the Keystone/106th roundabout. Incidentally, the school was also used as a church until 1852, when the White Chapel Methodist Church was established. Farley himself was buried in the Farley Cemetery when he died in 1856.

In his will, dated 1843, he asked that the 160 acres in the southeast quarter of the section be sold when his youngest son, Thomas, reached the age of fifteen and the money be split equally among the family. Farley outlived that deadline, and the family still owned much of the property in 1866, except for about 30 acres on the north side between the school and the cemetery, which had changed ownership to members of the McShane family.[27] According to aerial photos starting in the 1930s, this northern area was heavily wooded until the 1960s.

Any remnants of the park would likely be gone now. The land has changed townships as well; this was part of the section of Delaware Township that was annexed into Clay Township in the 1950s. It's unfortunate that the park didn't survive. When John Haines wrote his history of Hamilton County in 1915, he repeated the story and spoke regretfully about the missed opportunity. If the park had been kept to the present day, it would mean that there would be a section of old-growth forest in the Fishers/Carmel area.[28]

Part II

THE CHANGING LANDSCAPE

Floods

Probably the greatest flood in Indiana history was in 1913, and people talk about it as though it was a truly unique event. Yet of the top ten floods that have occurred in Hamilton County through its history, half of them have happened within the last twenty years. According to records at the National Weather Service, which go back to 1948,[29] the top list is:

(1) 23.80 feet on March 25, 1913
(2) 21.86 feet on July 10, 2003
(3) 21.31 feet on April 22, 1964
(4) 21.29 feet on December 31, 1990
(5) 21.00 feet on January 13, 2005
(6) 20.65 feet on May 14, 2002
(7) 20.55 feet on June 15, 1958
(8) 20.42 feet on January 24, 1999
(9) 20.07 feet on March 25, 2007
(10) 19.99 feet on September 4, 2003

For comparison, the lowest girders on the Logan Street bridge in Noblesville are at 26.05 feet. The 2003 crest was within 2.00 feet of the 1913 crest. The next ten highest have the same ratio:

(11) 19.94 feet on June 30, 1957
(12) 19.86 feet on March 1, 2011

Lake Erie and Western Railroad bridge in the 1913 flood. *Roberts Collection, Hamilton East Public Library.*

(13) 19.59 feet on January 7, 2005
(14) 19.43 feet on April 19, 2013
(15) 19.25 feet on December 24, 2013
(16) 19.20 feet on January 14, 2013
(17) 19.14 feet on February 25, 1985
(18) 19.11 feet on June 4, 1980
(19) 18.97 feet on January 5, 1950
(20) 18.96 feet on March 6, 1963

What's more, this list doesn't include floods prior to 1948. The flood that happened in January 1937 was a huge event nationally. However, the Noblesville newspaper said that the crest was at 19.00 feet, which was lower than the 22.00 feet measured in 1913. Transposing that to modern National Weather Service measurement would make the 1937 flood 20.80 feet—not even in the top five. The reports reflect that. At the time, the newspaper mostly talked about helping refugees from places that were hit worse.[30]

March 1904 saw a flood that is now completely forgotten. There is no record of its height, except what we are able to deduce from later references.

Noblesville neighborhood Johnstown in the 1913 flood. *Roberts Collection, Hamilton East Public Library.*

It was estimated that the 1904 flood level was 2.0 feet lower than 1913, making it similar to the 2003 level. This may have been high. The 1913 crest in Indianapolis was 4.4 feet higher than in 1904, and Anderson was 3.3 feet higher. Since Noblesville is roughly midway between those cities, the crest may have been somewhere between those numbers—perhaps around 20.0 feet. We do know that the cemetery was submerged and the Midland railroad bridge was destroyed.[31]

The newspaper compared the flood in 1904 to floods in 1872, 1847 and 1823. There is no record of an 1872 White River flood anywhere. The writer was possibly referring to one that occurred in June 1875. Again, there is no official measurement. We do know that it was lower than the recently built Potters Bridge and did a half million dollars' worth of damage (which would be equal to over $10 million today).[32]

The 1847 flood happened in January. Augustus F. Shirts shared his memories of the flood in his 1901 history of the county: "Shocks of corn and fodder, securely tied as it had been left in the fall before, were frequently seen floating down the river. I remember seeing a pig on one of these shocks floating past Noblesville. It was eating corn, apparently as unconcerned as it would have been in the barn lot at home. On another shock was a chicken floating quietly downstream." Shirts said a part of Riverside Cemetery was covered by the water. In the 1923 centennial issue of the *Noblesville Ledger*, Hugh Anthony Maker passed along stories told by Silas Hugh Moffitt, who witnessed the 1847 event. Moffitt surmised that 1913 was one or two feet higher than 1847, which would have made the earlier flood around twenty-one or twenty-two feet.[33]

In the same centennial issue, Maker passed on stories of the 1823 flood told to him by his grandmother. One story she told was of a cabin at Strawtown that had been built on the bottomland. Local Delaware Indians smiled as it was being constructed and pointed to marks on trees. The cabin builder realized what that meant when the flood came and the water rose to a few feet above the peak of the roof. Another story passed down was that William Conner had a mark somewhere on his property for the 1823 flood that was two and a half feet higher than the 1913 level, which would have made it around twenty-six feet!

Traces of the Canals

If you've read much Indiana history, you've heard about the attempts to build canals and the failures that resulted. One of the classic stories is that of the Central Canal, which now exists only in two sections between Broad Ripple and the Canal Walk in Indianapolis. However, there was also some digging done here in Hamilton County, traces of which may still be seen today.

The canal projects came about because of the Mammoth Internal Improvements Act of 1836 passed by the Indiana state legislature. This act was to build new transportation routes for settlers coming into the area. In the end, it created too many projects that were begun simultaneously and failed and ended with the state going bankrupt in 1839. The canals were still being discussed into the 1840s but were eventually abandoned. In his 1901 history of Hamilton County, Augustus Finch Shirts describes some excavation getting started in this area and says, "Evidence of this work is to be found at many points in the county."[34] So, what is left?

Maps show the route of the canal following the White River, and the first remnants can be found at Lafayette Trace Park. Aerial photos show a ditch that borders the park on two sides. Somewhere in this area was the proposed town of Chillicothe. According to a newspaper article, it was laid out in 1838 by Jonathan Hougham and David Provolt to take advantage of the canal. However, only seven lots were sold before the project failed.[35]

The canal route would have gone through Stephensburg (or Stevensburg), which was an early community near Strawtown. According to the 1866 map

Above: Route of Central Canal through Indiana. Detail from *Morse's North American Atlas* by Sidney Morse, 1842. *Library of Congress.*

Opposite: Map of Strawtown showing Canal Street. Detail from *Map of Hamilton Co., Indiana* by C.A.O. McClellan and C.S. Warner, 1866. *Hamilton County Surveyor's Office.*

of Hamilton County, Strawtown itself was supposed to have a Canal Street that would parallel or connect with the canal. It would have been roughly where one of the small roads connects Thirty-Seventh and Craig Streets. That area had originally been platted as the town of Woodville.[36]

Continuing south, an 1882 *Ledger* article said that a drainage ditch was being dug through Wayne Township along the old canal route, although it's not clear where that was. Wayne Township was where a quarry was established in 1836 for cutting stone blocks to use in bridges and aqueducts. After the canal failure, the stone was sold to use in buildings in town. Most of the evidence suggests the quarry may have been where Stony Creek crosses 191st Street near Union Chapel Road.[37]

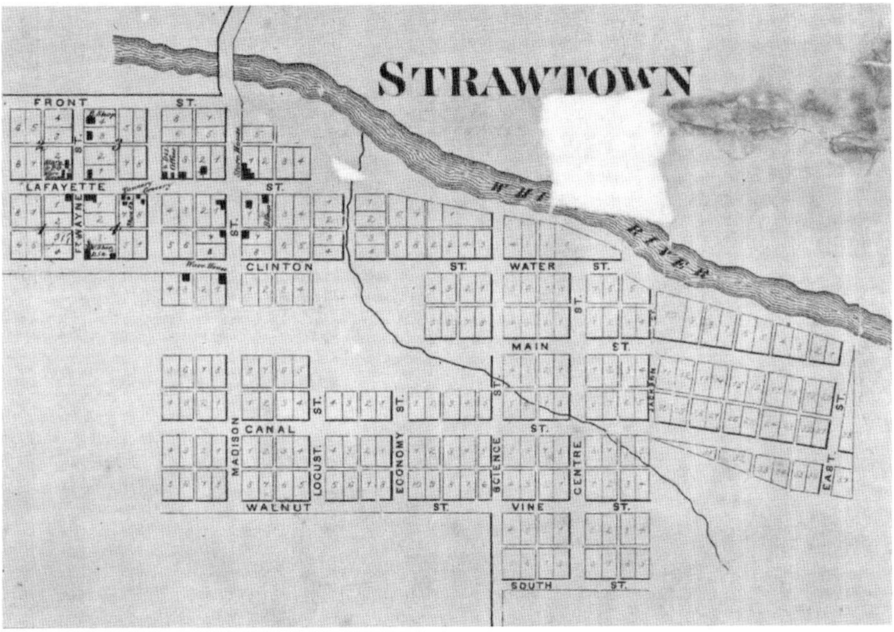

The most obvious remains of the canal are at the Meadows subdivision near the intersection of 191st Street and Highway 37. There is a historic marker on a street called Canal Way, and there are a series of parallel depressions in the ground that suggest canal locks. This may have been the site of the proposed town of Wheatley, which, according to another 1944 *Ledger* article, was laid out in 1839. Locks were built and land set aside for craftsmen, but it, too, failed and disappeared.[38]

For the town of Noblesville, Augustus Shirts talks about excavations being made and abandoned south of Conner Street. However, during a flood in 1847, he said the old ditches filled with water.[39] There is one artifact that remains in the area: a large stone block at Riverside Cemetery with "1824" carved on the side. The date was actually carved in the 1940s and is an error. However, as will be covered in Part VI, "The Riverside Cemetery Stone," the stone was originally to be used for a canal bridge or aqueduct and brought to the cemetery at a later time.

The canal route was to have continued south and have gone through Connerstown, the community around William Conner's trading post (now the site of Conner Prairie). It then would have eventually connected with the section built at Broad Ripple.

The 1850 Cholera Epidemic

The Noblesville cholera epidemic of 1850 was part of a worldwide cholera epidemic of the 1840s and 1850s. (A probable major factor in the spread of the disease was the growth of the British empire.) We have very little information about the Noblesville outbreak. The only newspaper account is a report in the *Evansville Daily Journal* on September 3, 1850, that said, "We learn that the cholera is prevailing to a considerable extent in Noblesville, in this state."

Most of the information that we have is from the 1901 history of Hamilton County by Augustus Finch Shirts. He was twenty-six years old at the time of the epidemic. According to Shirts, Patient Zero (as we would call him today) was Lucius H. Emmons, a forty-two-year-old former Noblesville newspaper editor who had been serving as a postal clerk in Washington, D.C. He had left his position and was returning to Noblesville to start a new newspaper. He came back to town via the Ohio River to Lawrenceburg and apparently contracted the disease there. He arrived in Noblesville on July 20 and died four days later, along with his one-year-old daughter, Abigail.[40] This was repeated in a report in the *Indiana State Sentinel* on August 1.

Shirts wrote in his history:

> *As soon as it became known that Mr. Emmons had been attacked by the cholera, fear and consternation overcame many of the good citizens of the town. Some of them made their way as soon as possible to the country; other remained away from where they supposed they would be likely to be infected*

> *by the disease.... It was a long time before people recovered from the shock. Aside from the fearful loss of life, the town suffered in the loss of trade. It was a long while before the people of the surrounding country could be induced to visit Noblesville.*

The outbreak seemed to run from July to September, but there is no precise data. Shirts identifies some of the victims by name in his book. Their ages and dates of death have been added.

Adolphus Hare, age one (son of Abraham), July 30
Andrew Passwater, age twenty-three, August 2
Daniel Hare, age thirty-six, August 3
Elizabeth Hare, age twenty-eight (wife of Daniel), August 3
Elizabeth F. Hare, age fifty-nine (mother of Daniel), August 3
Eliza Garver, age twenty-four, August 5
Julius Garver, age three (son of Eliza), August (no date)
Daniel W. Hare, age ten (son of Daniel), August 10
Abraham Hare, age twenty-eight (brother of Daniel, son of Elizabeth), August 10
Martha A. Ross, age twenty-nine, August 10

Other victims or possible victims include:

Nancy Mallory, age sixty-eight, August 19
Henry Cole, age one, September 3
Rebecca Ann Wilson, age four, September 18
Jane Reynolds, age eighteen, September 21

This information comes from Noblesville Township cemetery records, since most of the victims are buried in Riverside Cemetery. There may be more buried in other townships; Daniel Hare and his son were buried in White River Township.

The Noblesville population in 1850 was 664, which makes the 16 deaths into a 2.41 percent death rate for the city. The Noblesville Township population was 2,308, and the county population was 12,684. At the same time, Indianapolis suffered an estimated 50 cholera deaths out of a population of 8,091.

Shirts says that there was a second wave of the epidemic in 1853; however, we have no details regarding date, duration or deaths. Shirts simply says,

"The attack was not so fatal." Hamilton County went unmentioned in a report about cholera epidemics that was made for the Indiana State Medical Society in 1854.

A vaccine for cholera was not developed until the 1880s. However, by that time, society had found that what today would be considered basic hygiene was the best way to eliminate the virus.

In the end, the community survived, and the outbreak is forgotten today. Even at the time, it was not all grim. Despite people initially fleeing from the disease, Shirts wrote, "There were, however, many noble men and women who gave aid and comfort to the stricken ones during all their days of sorrow and trouble."

Ho for Noblesville!

The First Railroad

The first railroad into the county was incorporated on January 19, 1846, as the Peru and Indianapolis Railroad since its purpose was to connect the capital city with the Wabash and Erie Canal at Peru, which it did in 1854. The line was first constructed with what was called "flat bar rail" or "strap rail" or "slab track." While modern-style T rail was available, it was extremely expensive. (The best stuff was English and had to be imported.) So, the alternative was to secure wooden timbers along the ties and nail a heavy strip of iron to the top. This was a horrible solution, as the iron rails started to curl after a few trains ran over them. The part jutting up was called a "snakehead" and could punch a hole in an oncoming train. By the end of the 1850s, the strap rail along this line had been replaced with T rail.

All of the engines and cars used on the line at first were borrowed from the Madison and Indianapolis Railroad. There are no pictures of equipment on the line earlier than about 1900, although the company used woodcut illustrations in its advertising that give an idea of what it might have used. The small scale and low speed of these trains is why the line was put down the middle of Eighth (Polk) Street.

One story about the construction and unfamiliarity with the new technology involves a pioneer woman who was in the midst of making maple sugar. She was cooking a kettle of sap and left for a short time to do something else. Suddenly, she heard a loud, strange sound, which she

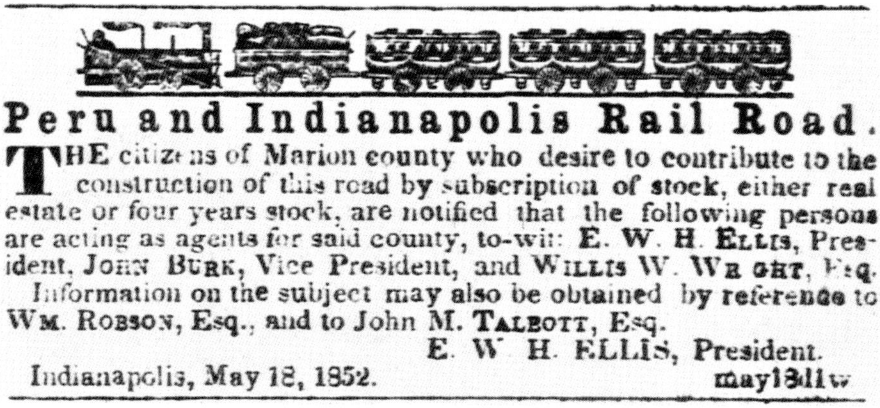

Peru and Indianapolis Railroad advertisement showing types of equipment. Indiana Daily Sentinel, *May 19, 1852.*

thought was the kettle boiling over. She checked in alarm and found that it was peacefully simmering. The sound was the screaming of the first steam whistle ever heard in Hamilton County.[41]

This venture was a catalyst for many things. Noblesville was incorporated as a town in January 1851, and the railroad reached town in March. When a celebration was planned on March 11 for the completion, the *Indiana State Sentinel* headlined the announcement "Ho for Noblesville!" The first train ran from Indianapolis to Noblesville at 8:00 a.m. and took about an hour and a half to get there. The train had open cars filled with all sorts of riders. We know the name of one of the original passengers was Sarah Summers. This fact was mentioned in her obituary when she died in 1908 at the age of ninety-three.[42]

In Noblesville, the streets were packed with people, with estimates of five thousand being in town that day. Brass bands from Indianapolis and Noblesville were playing. At 11:00 a.m., former Indiana governor David Wallace gave a speech. There are several accounts of the event. The *Sentinel* reported, "At every crossroad, crowds of anxious and astonished Hoosiers were waiting to get their first sight of the iron horse, and as he foamed and puffed along, we were greeted with cheering and waving of handkerchiefs." Cary Harrison, a resident of Noblesville, said in a letter, "Old settlers that used to travel deer paths and heard the howl of wolves and the screams of panthers now can have the whistle of the locomotive, the roaring of the cars, and the tolling of the bells." Indianapolis businessman Calvin Fletcher was pleased with the event but pointed out, "Some of the young men of

Indianapolis became intoxicated with liquor greatly to the grief of those who have regard to the character of the place."[43]

Fletcher, Wallace and several other important Indiana leaders spent part of the day at William Conner's house in Noblesville. The seventy-four-year-old Conner had given land to the railroad to build a station in Noblesville. At 4:00 p.m., three trains returned to Indianapolis from Noblesville. However, so many people were in town that there wasn't enough room on the trains for all of them, and many people had to spend the night in Noblesville.

In 1864, the line was reorganized as the Indianapolis, Peru and Chicago Railway and later went through several corporate identities. It was abandoned in 2018, and most of the tracks were removed.

Industrial Growth

Sheridan and Its Dirt

From Egbert Higbee's flour mill to the glass and brick works that sprang up during the natural gas boom, and from Wilson's Milk Factory to Biddle Precision Components today, the town of Sheridan has never been a stranger to business and industry. Among other things, inventor Homer K. Johnson of Sheridan filed a patent for a soybean harvester in 1922. When the Monon Railroad was constructed in 1882, it provided an outlet for the goods manufactured in the area. Through all of this, the most peculiar product ever shipped out of Sheridan was…dirt. Just to the northwest of the town is a patch of a particular kind of soil that turns out to be the best consistency for horse racing tracks. In 1891, a new harness track called the Hawthorne Race Course (which is still in business today) was being built west of Chicago.[44]

Approximately 900 railroad carloads of soil were excavated just northwest of the Sheridan town limits. Since a typical gondola car might carry fifty tons, the final total could have been as much as forty-five thousand tons of dirt. The excavation was visible into the 1920s. The Indiana humorist George Ade said about the track (tongue-in-cheek), "It was decided, after much investigation, that Indiana soil helped to encourage a high rate of speed." Following this, in 1892, the new Indiana State Fairgrounds was being built and needed soil for its track as well. As the Monon Railroad ran directly from Sheridan to the western border of the grounds, the choice seems obvious. One source stated that 1,100 carloads of soil were brought down the railroad line.[45]

Brickmaking in the County

When looking at the important structures of the county, there is a building material that many of them share: bricks. Bricks are, quite literally, the building blocks of the county. How they were made and where they were used says something about the history of the county.

The first brick building in the county was William Conner's house, built in 1823. Later historians said that common practice was to dry the molded clay in the sun, build a kiln to fire the bricks to the proper hardness and demolish the kiln after the job was done. The construction of the Conner house was followed in 1827 by the brick homes of Silas Moffitt, William Wilkerson and Zenas Beckwith. The first public brick building was the recorder's office, built in 1832.[46]

The business of brickmaking got started in 1840. William Stanbrough established the earliest known real brickyard in the county in Washington Township, where he built a kiln and sold bricks. Evidently, there was enough of a demand that Westfield resident Nathan Johnson was awarded a patent for a brick-making mold in 1854. In addition to brick, clay was used for drainage tiles to drain the swampy areas of the county. By 1869, tile factories had been established in Noblesville, Westfield and Carmel. There was a community in Washington Township named Tile Factory Corner. In 1880, Fishers had a tile factory on the main street in town.[47]

Brickmakers in Noblesville seemed to concentrate on Federal Hill along Stringtown Pike (present-day Lakeview Drive), possibly because of a clay deposit. There had been an attempt to establish a town called Garversville just west of the railroad along present Park Street, and the brickyards were usually in that area. Among the Federal Hill brickmakers was Allen Fisher, who advertised for "brick moulders" in 1874 and got the contract for the new jail in 1875. A successful gas well was drilled in 1887 on Federal Hill and was used to fire bricks. The R.L. Wilson house (293 South Eighth Street) had a sidewalk made with bricks from a natural gas kiln. However, people still reported seeing loads of wood taken to the kilns in 1890.[48]

In 1888, James Lawson began making brick on Federal Hill and became one of the more successful companies. He had a cousin in Indianapolis

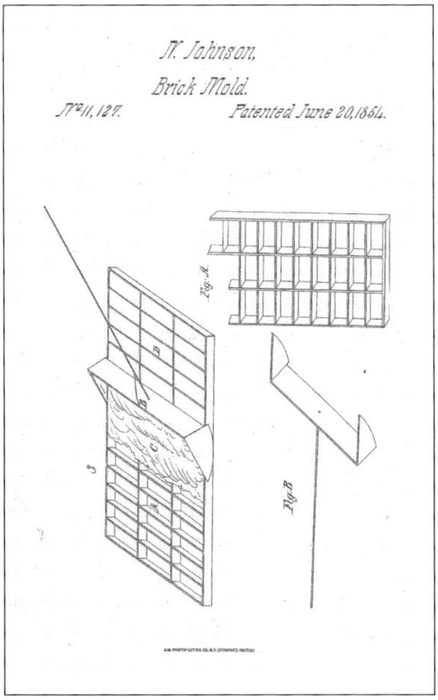

Nathan Johnson's patent for a brick mold, 1854. *U.S. Patent Office.*

who made terra-cotta ornaments for buildings. Terra cotta was used on some buildings in Noblesville; it can be seen as plaques on the Harris-Joseph block (2 North Ninth Street). It was also used for animal head decorations on the Northside Block, which burned in 1957. Lawson made bricks for sewers, the Strawboard factory, the Carbon Works and the Cicero glass factory. Some Lawson brick buildings still standing are the Lacy/Knights of Pythias building (848 and 856 Logan Street) and the Red Men's Lodge (101 North Tenth Street).[49]

Sheridan had its own tile and brick factories in the 1870s and 1880s run by people like Eli Hiatt, William and Barney Fristoe and Henry Thistlewaite.

Apparently, there were limits to the local brickmakers' abilities. When the new county courthouse was being built in 1878–79, it was done with brick bought from the Peerless Brick Company in Philadelphia. Allen Fisher later said that he had supplied some of it. When Mayor James Worth Smith began paving the streets of Noblesville in 1894, the bricks were not local but were purchased from Brazil, Indiana. There was some discussion in the paper about not supporting local business.[50] Around this time, the citizens of Sheridan also began to pave their streets with brick.

Eventually the brickyards closed, although it's not clear if this was from a lack of material from all of the clay mining, a lack of fuel after the gas failed or a lack of demand as the boom faded. In 1907, Arcadia had the last real brick factory in the county, which was destroyed by fire that year.

Shooting Gas Wells

When discussing Hamilton County gas boom history, people are aware of the many industries (glass, brick, etc.) that grew up because of natural gas discoveries. What is often overlooked is the first step in the process—that is, getting the natural gas. Exploring this topic leads to several questions. Where did the gas come from? How did they go about getting it? What happened to all of it?

Geologically speaking, the roots of the boom start in a seabed that covered the state of Indiana millions of years ago. As time passed, the sediment from this seabed turned into limestone, and the plants and other natural items on the floor of the sea were trapped in pockets of the rock. This organic material eventually broke down into natural gas. The area that was heaviest in these pockets became known as the Trenton field and covered much of northeastern Indiana. Hamilton County was on the very southwestern edge.

Some of the gas pockets were near to the surface. The first discovery of gas in the county was in the 1830s or 1840s, before anyone really knew what to do with it. Ezekiel Clampitt, a farmer in Clay Township, was hand digging a well for water when he heard an odd noise, described as "buzzing." He climbed quickly out of the well (which was a very good thing) but then decided to investigate the noise. With his wife watching on one side and a neighbor on the other, he lowered a bucket with a candle in it down into the darkness of the well. Of course, the well erupted in flame. Clampitt and his wife were knocked to the ground, and the neighbor, who was wearing a nice linen suit, had his clothing set on fire. Fortunately, no one was seriously injured. Clampitt left this jet of flame burning for some time, and many visitors came by to see it. Eventually, he reburied it and dug another water well nearby.[51]

The first commercial discoveries came in the 1880s, when there was technology to use the gas. The first well in the state was found near Eaton in September 1886. The first wells in Hamilton County were drilled in 1887, with the first successful one being found at Noblesville in January. It was at what today is the corner of Eleventh and Pleasant Streets. It was ignited so that people could visit and admire the flow of gas and, ironically, was left to burn for a few months until it was figured out how to cap a high-pressure well. In April of that year, the largest well in the county was found: the Wainwright Wonder, located on the Wainwright farm on North Tenth Street in Noblesville. Gas was struck 850 feet below the surface and came out at a pressure of 800 psi (pounds per square inch). The pressure blasted chunks of the surrounding limestone rock up from the well. It, too, was left open for several months.[52]

The newspapers said the gas was found between 350 and 2,300 feet below the ground. The process involved a derrick and a rotary drill, drilling through dirt and gravel until the Trenton limestone was reached. At that point, in order to crack the rock, nitroglycerine was used. This was called "shooting a well" and involved large amounts of explosive. For example, in 1903, sixteen quarts were used to shoot a well on Harrison Street in Noblesville. The nitroglycerine was poured into a tin tube about five feet long and five inches in diameter called a "shell" or "torpedo," which was sealed and lowered into the well. Then a heavy, pointed piece of iron called a "go-devil" was dropped into the mouth of the well, and everyone quickly walked away. A few seconds later, there would be a rumble and a spout of dirt that would, hopefully, be followed by a rush of gas.[53]

As might be imagined, there could be problems with this method. A well being drilled near New Britton in 1904 ran into a layer of rock thought to be very thick. One shell was filled with twenty quarts of nitroglycerine and was lowered into the well on a rope as another shell of the same size was being filled. Suddenly, the rope on the first one came untied, and the shell dropped rapidly down the well. The crew fled for their lives and managed to reach a safe distance before the shell landed. The extent of the damage is not known, but the crew said the explosion was "very loud."[54]

The natural gas boom went bust surprisingly quickly. One of the main reasons was that promoters would do public displays by lighting the gas flowing from a well and leaving it to burn. This was their way of claiming to have an infinite amount of gas. Tourists would come and visit these fields of flaming wells. Despite warnings from geologists, they continued to do this until there was a noticeable loss in the pressure. The gas boom ended in Hamilton County around 1905–10. While gas was occasionally found later, the large commercial wells failed. It was the end of a very distinctive period in Hamilton County history.

The Strawboard Fish Kill

The White River at Noblesville had pollution problems from the earliest days of settlement. The first industry in town was Cogswell's tannery (now the site of the judicial center), which poured waste products into the river in the 1830s. Throughout the nineteenth century, refuse from the livery stables along Conner Street flowed straight into the river.

The situation worsened with the industrial growth that came with the 1887 gas boom. One of the first factories that sprang up was the American Strawboard Company plant, which made a type of cheap cardboard from straw. The straw would be broken down with muriatic acid and re-formed. It was good for packing glassware, another growth industry. In later years, the plant would be purchased by Ball Brothers.[55]

The plant was constructed in 1889 and was supposed to be one of the largest in the world. It was built in southwest Noblesville, becoming a big employer in the area and causing a growth of housing. The nickname of the area changed from the natural beauty of "Plum Prairie" to gritty "Johnstown" after the 1889 flood in Pennsylvania.[56]

Indiana had already been having problems with strawboard plants polluting rivers, so the state inspected the site in December 1890. While it was declared favorable, there were complaints about water quality by March 1891. The plant continued to run full throttle, beating the national record for production in April—one ton an hour for a thirty-six-hour run.[57]

In 1893, the Indianapolis Water Company had enough of worrying about its supply of water and brought a lawsuit. It complained that there was constant leakage from the refuse ponds where the acid-soaked waste was left to settle. The strawboard company agreed to a compromise and ceased running to upgrade the reservoir. The locals were upset that 150 men were put out of work by this. The plant eventually reopened, but the newspaper stories about pollution continued.[58]

The long-feared event finally happened on May 30, 1896. The levee between the refuse ponds and the river washed out, releasing an enormous amount of toxic waste. From Noblesville to Broad Ripple, the shore was lined with dead fish. People thought at first that poisons killed the fish, but a scientist later explained that a chemical reaction was taking oxygen out of the water, and the fish were actually suffocating.[59]

The plant worked quickly to repair the break, but the damage was done. Citizens in Indianapolis were alarmed about their drinking water supply. It was primarily drawn from wells, but river water was occasionally used. Some restaurants began hauling water from elsewhere.[60]

In June, another lawsuit between the Indianapolis Water Company and the strawboard company came to court. Addison Clay Harris represented the water company. Harris had a personal interest, in that he and his wife had purchased land in 1880 at Allisonville Road and 96th Street for a summer home. They were in the midst of refurbishing the house there. (That structure would eventually become an event center called the Ambassador House.) Since the house was very close to the river, they probably had seen and smelled dead fish. The strawboard company was represented by John W. Kern, who later ran for vice president with William Jennings Bryan and became a U.S. senator from Indiana.[61]

Site of the break in the embankment at the Strawboard factory that caused the fish kill. Indianapolis News, *June 2, 1896.*

One witness—George Black from Fishers Station—said that he was at the river that day and noticed the water rise, get dark and start smelling bad. He saw fish trying to jump out of the river and many just turning belly up. He caught some, but they were dead or dying, and he didn't eat them.

Another witness—Dr. John N. Hurty of the State Board of Health—went to Noblesville soon after the break to investigate the strawboard ponds. He said the break in the levee was eighty feet long and the ponds were empty of water. While he was there, the superintendent of the plant came out and confronted him, saying that Hurty was no gentleman and should have come to see him in the daytime. He also called him a "dirty, stinking pup." Hurty organized an effort to clean out the river and removed about five tons of fish, which were so rotten that the men working got sick.

Eventually, the court decided that the strawboard company was in contempt of the previous injunction to improve the reservoir. A fine was levied against the plant of $250 and costs. This is a small amount, but there was not much else the court could do. There were few official laws about pollution. By October, the strawboard company had purchased more acreage and was building larger refuse ponds.[62]

The Noblesville strawboard plant ran until the 1960s. While older community residents talk about the smell from the place, there are no more reports of a similar breach.

Some Hamilton County Inventors

A Woman Inventor

Alice Armstrong (1813–1901) was from Noblesville, and in 1891, she invented a kind of window latch. The latch was controlled by a spring and could lock the window at different heights. She was a Quaker and apparently rather independent-minded. She outlasted two husbands and didn't take the name of the second one. In 1894, at the age of eighty-one, she had her own business selling music. She is buried at Hinkle Creek Cemetery.[63]

A Unique Machine Gun

Thomas R. Cook (1833–1918) was a machinist in Noblesville when he invented a type of machine gun in 1889. Cook had been an inventor for a while. He had filed articles of incorporation for the Cook Automatic Gate Company in June 1879, and his occupation was listed in the 1880 census as "selling automatic gates." However, according to the *Indianapolis News*, he didn't have a patent for the gate until 1884. He was listed in the 1886, 1887 and 1889 Indianapolis city directories as the president of the Cook Automatic Gate Company and was living in rooming houses.

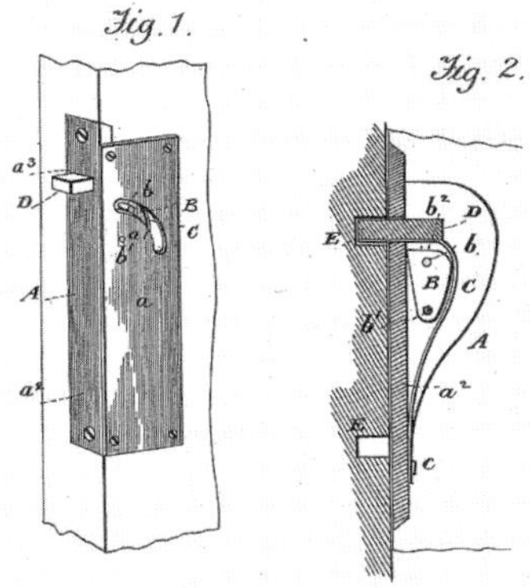

Left: Alice Armstrong's latch patent, 1891. *U.S. Patent Office.*

Right: Newspaper image of Thomas Cook standing at the back of his machine gun. Indianapolis News, *September 19, 1891.*

He got his patent for the gun in 1891. There was a one-third share in the patent for Henry Caylor, a Noblesville businessman who had probably funded the research and construction of a model. An *Indianapolis News* article about the gun says that Cook was living in Irvington in 1891. It stated that he had developed the gun after being an infantryman in the Civil War.[64]

There was an article published in the *New Orleans Times-Democrat* in 1889, when Cook first applied for the patent. It said that the Cook gun had one barrel, unlike the more famous Gatling gun patented in 1862. However, the image of the Cook gun in the 1891 *Indianapolis News* article shows it having multiple barrels. Gatling developed his multiple-barrel gun because a single barrel got too hot and would become fouled with burned powder residue. Improved metallurgy and smokeless powder eventually ended that concern. The Maxim gun invented in 1883 also had a single barrel, but the barrel was surrounded by a metal jacket that was to be filled with water to cool it during firing.[65]

The Indianapolis and New Orleans newspaper articles about the Cook machine gun said that it could fire one thousand rounds a minute. This was very impressive since, at that time, the Gatling gun and the Maxim gun did about six hundred rounds per minute. The newspaper articles also said that Cook had developed a smaller version of the gun to be used in railway express cars that carried mail and money being transferred. The gun was to be placed in an interior corner of the car, and if train robbers broke into the car, the train crew would stand behind a metal plate and fire away.

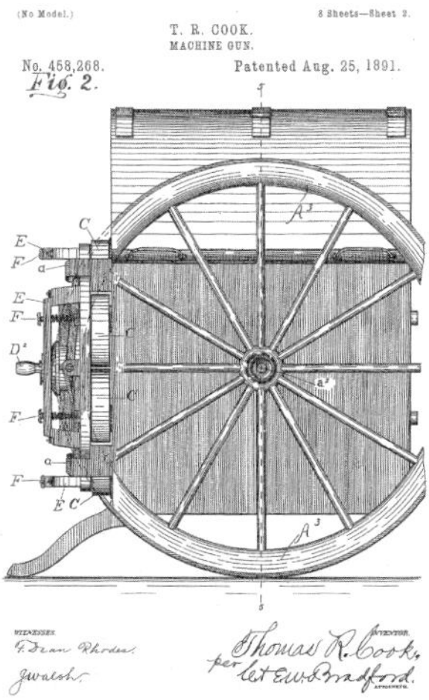

Left: One drawing from Thomas A. Cook's machine gun patent, 1891. *U.S. Patent Office.*

Right: Newspaper image of the front of the Cook machine gun. Indianapolis News, *September 19, 1891.*

Despite all of this, there is no evidence that the Cook gun was ever manufactured or used. The machinery may have been too complex; it took a three-man crew to run it. The Gatling and Maxim were comparatively simpler. Cook continued to make improvements on the gun and was issued a second patent in 1896.[66] He is buried in Crown Hill Cemetery in Arcadia.

A YOUNG INVENTOR

A young man named George McDonald (1880–1947) set a high bar for homebuilt science experiments. Although he spent most of his life as a farmer in Wayne Township, as a teenager, he developed an astronomical model and received a patent for it.

According to the *Hamilton County Democrat* of April 23, 1897:

> *George, son of Jacob McDonald, who lives nine miles northeast of this city, has secured a patent on a Tellurian, or Globe apparatus, which is one of the most complete Globes now extant. Mr. McDonald invented his apparatus in his 13th year, and for a time let it rest, but instituted proceedings for a patent, which he has secured. We have not time to give a full description of*

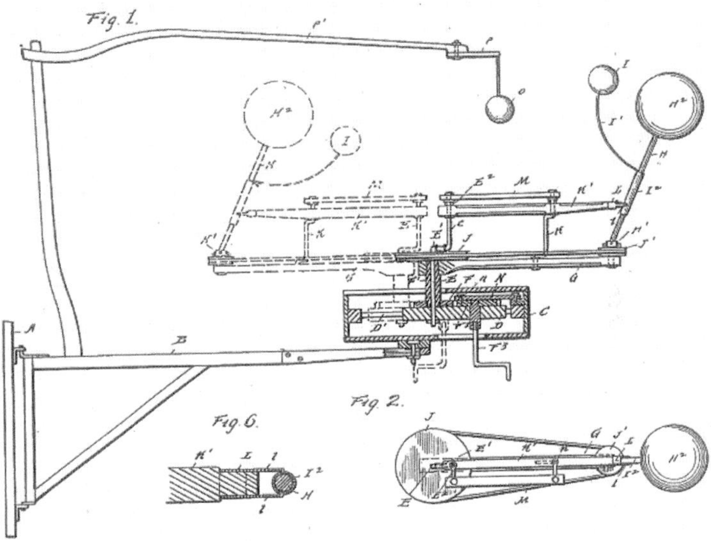

John and George MacDonald's patent for Tellurian, 1897. *U.S. Patent Office.*

> *this Globe, but will say, that the boy, for he is only 16 years old now, shows considerable skill as an inventor.*

A tellurian (sometimes spelled tellurion) is a model showing the relative motion of the Earth, moon and sun. When a crank is turned, the ball representing the Earth rotates around the ball representing the sun while tilting on its axis, and the ball representing the moon rotates around the Earth. The device is primarily an educational tool for demonstrating planetary movement. A model of the solar system that includes all of the planets is called an orrery.

The description in the patent says:

> *Be it known that we, Jacob McDonald and George McDonald, citizens of the United States, and residents of Wayne Township, in the county of Hamilton and the State of Indiana, have invented new and useful Improvements in Tellurians; and we do declare the following to be a full, clear, and exact description of the invention, such as will enable others skilled in the art to which it appertains to make and use the same, reference being had to the accompanying drawings, and to letters of reference marked thereon, which form a part of this specification.*

> *The object of this invention is to provide a tellurian of improved character wherein the various movements of the earth and moon with respect to the sun and to each other may be clearly illustrated, the mechanism employed being of simple character and not likely to become deranged.*[67]

His father was probably listed in the patent because George was too young to make a legal contract. Making and patenting tellurians was not unusual for the time. The patent office has records of several similar items dating to the same period.

George was evidently a good scholar. He graduated from Wayne Township schools in June 1898 and gave an address at the commencement titled "Habits and Their Influence." The speech was well received, and he was chosen to represent the township graded schools at the county oratorical contest later that month.

Reverse Fracking: The Castor Water Pump

There is a lot of discussion these days about fracking, the process of using water combined with other substances to make a special fluid that can force oil out of the ground. In 1889, a Wayne Township man reversed that concept and invented a system to use the pressure from natural gas wells to force water out of the ground, which, while the gas pressure lasted, seemed to be a great success.

William H. Castor (1834–1912) and Samuel B. Castor (1838–1907) were brothers and the sons of John H. Castor, who moved to Hamilton County in 1834. William was a farmer and one of the organizers of the Anderson, Lebanon and St. Louis Railroad (known as the Midland Railroad). Samuel was a teacher and a farmer and laid out the town of Durbin.

When William was on the board of directors of the railroad, it suffered financial problems, and he ended up losing $30,000. He went bankrupt in 1878, just after the line had reached Noblesville. He then left the railroad business and worked on rebuilding his fortunes. The *Noblesville Ledger* of August 26, 1881, said, "W.H. Castor has made his house to correspond with the illustration in the county history. It did not till now and appears quite palatial." In June 1883, the *Ledger* said that he had ordered lumber to build the largest barn in the county, which would be ninety feet by one hundred feet and thirty feet to the eaves.

The 1887 gas boom brought prosperity back to the family, particularly after wells were drilled on their land. William's farm became known for its use of gas. The *Ledger* for September 9, 1887, said that the house was all piped for heat and light, with a patent gas feed regulator and four lawn burners (large outdoor gaslights). The article said that he was planning to put in hot and cold running water, as well as run gas to the butchering house and the wash house.

Then Samuel came up with an idea to get maximum use from the gas. Powerful wells had enormous pressure from the escaping gas; a brick dropped into one would fly back out and be thrown very far. Samuel thought that this kinetic energy from the initial pressure could be used as a source of power in and of itself.

The *Hamilton County Democrat* of June 22, 1888, announced, "S.B. Castor is the inventor of a pump that will revolutionize the pump business. It will throw water from wells, no difference how deep they are. Patent applied for. We will tell more about the wonderful pump in the near future."

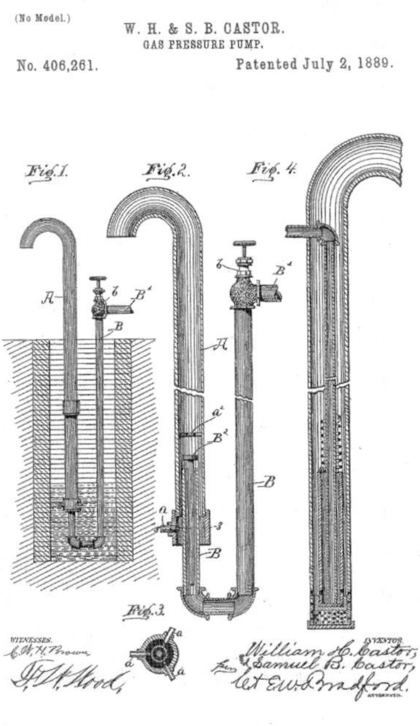

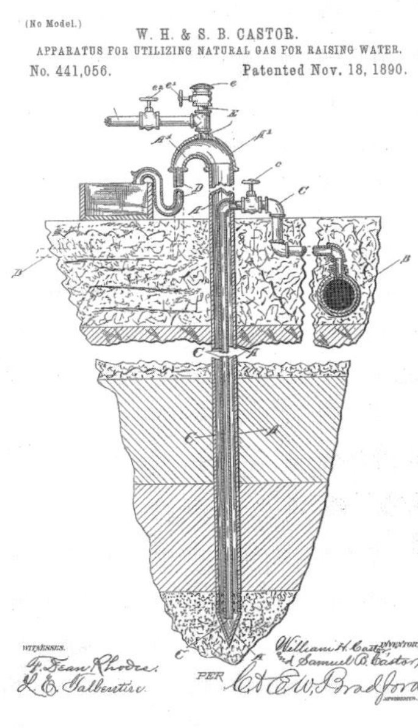

Left: W.H. and S.B. Castor's patent for gas pressure water pump, 1889. *U.S. Patent Office.*

Right: W.H. and S.B. Castor's patent for apparatus for using natural gas for raising water, 1890. *U.S. Patent Office.*

In July 1889, the brothers were granted a patent for a pump that could be used in something small like a cistern. A gas pipe would be run into the well and back up into the water pipe, with the joint between them below the water level. When the gas was turned on, the pressure would cause suction, drawing the water up the water pipe to the surface. It's apparent that the idea of mixing the gas and the water didn't bother anyone in the least.[68]

The *Democrat* said on August 2, 1889, "If you want to see how natural gas can be utilized for everything except eating, take a drive out to W.H Castor's farm—fish ponds, fountains, watering stock, heating, lighting, running saw mills, &c."

The brothers received a patent for another pump in November 1890. This version went deep underground, drawing on the natural water table. It was an improved model since you would be able to tap off the gas afterward and use it for fuel. It was actually given a practical application at a local business.[69]

An article in the *Ledger* on May 29, 1891, said, "Wm. and S.B. Castor began this morning a second water well for the Electric Light company, in White River. The well will be a few feet in the river and will be sunk to a depth of thirty-five feet. In the well will be placed one of Castor's patent natural gas pumps, which will force the water up the hill to the boiler in the dynamo house."

The gas pressure began to fail within a few years, and by 1895, the gas companies were struggling to keep the supply flowing. A pressurized apparatus like this would be useless. The brothers moved on to other things, and the Patented Castor Water Pump was relegated to being an industrial curiosity.

The Wilson Windmill

Richard Walter Wilson, known as R. Walter or just R.W., was born in 1873 to a Quaker farm family near Westfield. In 1905, he created a system to get steady electrical power from windmills. A windmill, of course, does not run at the constant speed that's required by a dynamo. (Now computers are used to deal with this.) His system was mechanical and based on the flow of water pumped by a windmill into a water tank and then released at a steady pace. There was also a back-up battery bank that would be steadily recharged. A key part of the system was a

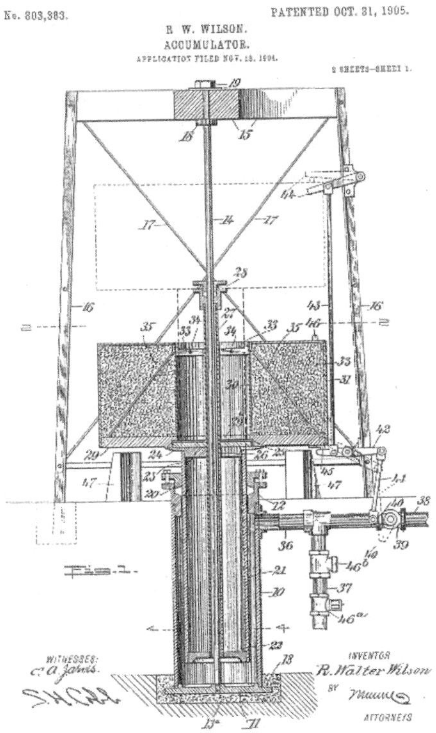

Walter Wilson's patent for the "accumulator" for making wind-powered electricity. *U.S. Patent Office.*

device called an "accumulator" in the patent application and called a "regulator" in media reports.

The patent description for the accumulator says:

> *My invention relates to apparatus for storing energy and regulating its application, it being particularly adapted for use in connection with such motors of irregular speed such as windmills which are applied to the pumping of water. Its principal objects are to provide automatic means for controlling the reception and delivery of energy by the accumulator and to generally improve the construction of apparatus of this class.*[70]

There was extensive media coverage on this in newspapers and magazines. The magazine *Technical World* reported, "This simple harness, once put in operation, will virtually run itself, requiring little or no attention. Mr. Wilson demonstrated the success of the invention at his own shop in Westfield, which is brightly lighted with wind-made electricity, and to all appearances it equals the steam-made product that city folk enjoy."[71]

Complete Lighting Set Consisting of Regulator, Water Motor, Dynamo, and Storage Battery.

Photograph of Wilson's system installed. Scientific American, *June 1, 1907.*

The Water Pumped by the Windmill is Delivered Through a Regulator to a Water Motor Which Drives the Electric Generator.

Drawing of Wilson's system in the house. Scientific American, *June 1, 1907.*

The magazine *Our Day* said, "There is no doubt that Mr. Wilson has solved the problem of a steady light, and that, with his invention, houses and barns supplied by it can be lighted for three or four days at a time even if there is a dead calm and the windmill does not make a single revolution."[72]

An article in *Scientific American* was a little more skeptical: "Mr. R.W. Wilson of Noblesville, Ind., seems to have reached a successful solution of the question, at least as far as the requirements of his own home are concerned."[73]

A company was formed in Noblesville in June 1906 called the Wind Mill Electric Company (capital stock $20,000) for the purpose of manufacturing this system. The company got a Canadian patent for the accumulator in October. This was a good year for Wilson; he was married in September.[74]

Evidently, the company didn't work out, however. Maybe like some tech start-ups today, Wilson was too much ahead of the curve and there was not enough demand. Nothing is known about it after this, and Wilson had moved to Los Angeles by 1910, where he lived for the rest of his life.

The Fodrea-Malott Beetle Flyer

The company was established in Noblesville, and the most likely date is 1908–9. It was the brainchild of two men: William L. Fodrea (born 1872) and Charles K. Malott (born 1889). Both were from families with some standing in the community. Malott's father was a livestock buyer. Charles himself made his living as a chauffeur, which at that time meant anyone who was hired out to drive an automobile. Many car owners weren't mechanically knowledgeable.

However, knowing about machines and knowing about business are two different things. In June 1909, a pretty chorus girl hired Charles to drive her from Noblesville to Chicago. When they arrived, she paid him with a check—which turned out to be one of many she had forged. He got his money back when she was arrested later.[75]

His partner, William Fodrea, was very mechanically oriented. He received at least six patents between 1906 and 1927. His father was county recorder, and his sister was one of the most popular teachers in Noblesville. However, William probably kept to the background in the business dealings of the company. He had been arrested for murder in January 1901 when an alleged romantic rival was found shot in the head with a shotgun. The trial attracted a great deal of attention, particularly since the main witness against him was one of the town's most notorious prostitutes. Her lack of credibility worked to his advantage, and in June 1902, the jury found him not guilty. At one point in the trial, in order to support his respectable reputation, it was mentioned that he had tinkered with engines ever since he was a small child.[76]

The impetus for the car company may have been Fodrea's 1906 patent application for a new kind of vehicle transmission. The first and only vehicle for the company was christened the "Beetle Flyer." The factory was set up in the carriage shed of the Malott family home at Fifteenth and Grant Streets. There is a possibility that there were as many as eight employees. These people are listed in the 1908 city directory as working for an automobile maker. This was happening before Henry Ford developed the concept of the assembly line, so the cars would have been built by hand and one at a time.

An *Indianapolis Star* article from July 13, 1908, states:

> *"The Beetle Flyer" was in the city last week, and everywhere it stopped a crowd gathered and marveled. People thought it was wonderful and they said so. Just exactly what the "Beetle Flyer" was puzzled the crowds at first, but the inventor, W.L. Fodrea of Noblesville, was one of the passengers in the home-made automobile, and he explained the workings of the machine to the curious.*
>
> *The automobile which Fodrea and Charles K. Malott constructed is the result of about five years' study and work. Fodrea explained that with this machine attached to any buggy or carriage, an automobile could be made within a short time. All that is necessary, he explained, is to place a small gasoline engine on the front of the vehicle bed, place the front wheels ahead of the engine, and attach some machinery to the rear wheels, and a motor buggy is the result. It is the intention of Fodrea and Malott to make their invention a useful addition to a farm.*
>
> *They say that a farmer can provide himself with an attachment for his buggy and have an automobile, or that he can utilize the power in the gasoline engine to run a pump, a grindstone, or anything else about the farm that he wants propelled by motor power.*

What may have caused the company to fold was a mishap by Charles Malott. The practice at the time was to purchase parts for the vehicles from other manufacturers and bring them to Noblesville to be put together. In early December 1909, Malott was driving an automobile loaded with tires

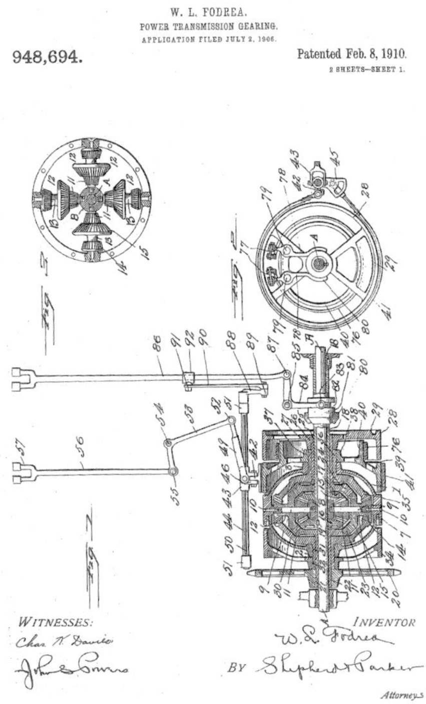

Right: William Fodrea's patent for transmission, 1906. *U.S. Patent Office.*

Below: Interior photograph of Fodrea-Malott workshop on Grant Street, Noblesville. Horseless Carriage Gazette, *July–August 1969.*

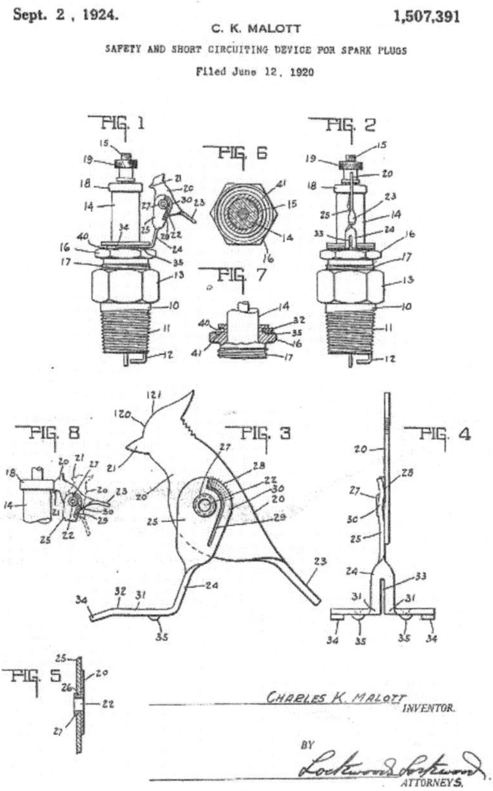

Charles Malott's patent for sparkplug safety device, 1924. *U.S. Patent Office.*

and supplies on Kentucky Avenue in Indianapolis when suddenly, the car caught on fire. While Charles was uninjured, the vehicle was destroyed and most of the supplies were burned. Most sources agree that the company disappeared soon after this. Henry Ford began producing his Model T in 1908, and it would have been difficult for Fodrea-Malott to compete with a ready-to-go, cheap, reliable vehicle.[77]

William Fodrea later moved to Little Rock, Arkansas, and continued to work on mechanical devices. Charles Malott eventually moved to California. After the partnership broke up, both men continued to experiment and invent. Fodrea patented an automobile gearing system in 1914, an adjustable bicycle seat post in 1920 and a machine for working wire in 1924. In 1924, Malott patented a safety device for sparkplugs. Curiously, the part to short circuit the sparkplug is shaped like a cardinal. Malott also patented a testing device for electrical systems in 1932.

Part III

DIVERSITY AND GROWTH

Catholicism in Early Hamilton County

Of the first wave of immigration into the county in the 1830s, a notable group of people were Catholic. They were largely from Ireland and Germany (although this predated the Irish famine of 1845–49 and the 1848 German revolutions). The groups were focused in the Mullen settlement in Jackson Township—with the Mullen, Meehan and Connelly families—and the Buscher settlement in White River Township. Both settlements were in proximity to the Lafayette Trace. Some of these people may have worked on the Central Canal project described earlier.[78]

When the gas boom began in 1887, the need for workers was filled by immigrants. A Noblesville Catholic church was organized in 1889 as St. Vincent de Paul, and a church building was constructed on South Ninth Street. Within ten years, the gas boom began to fail and the factories began to close down. The Noblesville church dissolved sometime after 1899, and the building was moved, cut in half and turned into tenant houses.[79]

A new Catholic church building was constructed in Cicero in January 1901. The Noblesville congregation went there to worship. It is now the Sacred Heart Church. Noblesville's second Catholic church, Our Lady of Grace, was organized in 1945.[80]

The Levinson Family

An important family in the growth of Noblesville was the Levinson family. The patriarch, Newman David Levinson (1832–1899), emigrated from Germany during the revolutions of 1848. He was usually called by his initials, N.D. The family stayed at first in Cincinnati, where N.D. met and married Mariah Newman, commonly known as Minnie.[81]

Eventually, N.D. decided to find a territory for his own business. It's not known what motivated his choices, but he came to Indiana. In 1851, the first railroad heading north from Indianapolis had been built, which led to Hamilton County and the town of Noblesville. Levinson arrived in 1857, after the community had been incorporated as a town for only six years.

He established a tailor shop and lived above it but was soon into clothing sales and purchased a house in which to raise his family. He moved the store into one section of a building built in 1866 on Conner Street. He was very successful and eventually purchased the entire building, enlarging it in 1884 and renaming it "the Grand."[82]

The Levinsons were one of the few Jewish families in town. N.D. would close the store for religious holidays, and a traveling rabbi from Indianapolis would attend to their spiritual needs. After their deaths, most of the family members were buried in a Jewish cemetery in Chicago.[83]

N.D. was highly respected in the community and was involved in politics and local fraternal organizations. He contributed letters to the newspaper under the pen name of Citizen. Minnie was greatly admired for her work

Left: Newman D. Levinson. Noblesville High School newspaper. Levinson Hamiltonian, *November 1917.*

Right: Minnie Levinson. Noblesville High School newspaper. Levinson Hamiltonian, *November 1917.*

with the Ladies' Aid Society and the library and her general charity work. Her kindness and generosity made her genuinely loved. Years later, in the 1940s, when a reporter did a story about the family, a bartender in the rough part of town told the reporter that he would "knock his block off" if the reporter was disrespectful of Mrs. Levinson. Another rough character said, "No better woman ever lived than Minnie Levinson."[84]

The family continued with local charity work after Newman's death in 1899 and Minnie's death in 1901. They had two sons, Salmon Oliver (known as Sol) and Harry. Sol started by donating money to Noblesville High School for a scholarship prize called the Levinson Award. This was first given out in 1906 and continues to be awarded today. Both sons contributed substantial funds for the Masonic temple in 1915. Their father had been a member of the group for many years, and his photograph still hangs prominently in the building.[85]

In 1916, the high school was officially named Levinson High School in honor of Newman and Minnie. This name was used for over thirty years, and the school newspaper was called the *Levin-Sun*. Both brothers were sports fans and gave money for a new high school gymnasium in 1924 and money

Left: Salmon O. Levinson. *Noblesville High School Annual, 1907.*

Right: Harry Levinson. Noblesville High School newspaper. Levinson Hamiltonian, *November 1917.*

to create Forest Park and its golf course in 1927. This was the first city park in Noblesville. The Eighth Street site of the family home was given to the city in 1932 for a city building. The spot is presently part of the site of the five-story Levinson Building.[86]

Much of this generosity was due to the success of Salmon. He was a graduate of Yale and became a very prominent Chicago lawyer. He was nominated for the Nobel Peace Prize in 1929 for his antiwar work.[87]

Harry ran the clothing business after the death of his father. He married local woman Nettie Kinsey in 1891, at a ceremony presided over by the Methodist minister. Her family were farmers who had moved to the county just after the Civil War and created a community called Kinsey's Corners south of Noblesville.[88] Harry and Nettie's first son, Frank, was born in 1894, and their second son, Norman David Levinson, was born on April 20, 1900.

Norman would later change his name to "Norell" and become a fashion designer. When he died in 1972, the *New York Times* called him the "Dean of American Fashion." He liked to say that his fashion interest started early. He would tell a story about riding in a baby carriage on Courthouse Square and throwing a fit until his mother had bought herself a new hat with cherries that he had seen in the window of Sowerwine Dry Goods.[89]

In November 1962, he had an opportunity to express his fond remembrances of his birthplace. In an October article about him, a fashion writer named Agnes McCoy referred to Noblesville as a little-known place and said that it was a surprise that someone as sophisticated as Norell had come from there. This was reprinted in the *Noblesville Ledger*, which Frank sent to Norman. Norman immediately wrote this to the *Ledger*:

> *I must say I resent Agnes McCoy saying Noblesville isn't important! However, it may be my fault because when someone asks me where I was born, I always say, "a very small town, Noblesville, Indiana." I always see it the same size it was when I was born there in 1900. It is quite willful because my memories of Noblesville are very precious to me. I still see the courthouse square with horses and buggies tied up around—Caylor's, Sowerwine's, Lowther's, the corner drug store, were all on the square (that was the town). Hare's Buggy store and John Dold's candy store were around the corner. Band concerts were held on Thursday night. The covered bridge was north of the square. So many wonderful happy memories. This is the way I think of Noblesville. I know perfectly well it isn't like this now. Maybe I do not like the passing of time. Whatever it is, my Noblesville is very important to me, whether Agnes McCoy thinks so or not.*[90]

Norman spent his first years in Noblesville and was precocious enough to remember them. However, in 1906, Harry wanted to expand the business and moved to Indianapolis. Harry was a serious baseball fan and had followed the Indianapolis team on a tour of cities to look at possible sites. The Harry Levinson stores were successful, and the company lasted for nearly a century.

A Vaquero in Hamilton County

While it's not known when the first immigrants from Latin America arrived in Hamilton County, there is some information about the first known Mexican visitor. We don't know much about him except for what was written in the newspapers, but he left quite an impression while he was here. The following is from the *Ledger* of June 1, 1877. (Warning: some of the language and the ways of treating animals are not in keeping with what we would do today.)

A HANDY MAN

A young Mexican, who wields the lasso and rattles the bones, has entertained the people on the streets with his dexterous manipulations, especially of the lasso, capturing dogs and halting boys in their headlong career by gracefully throwing about their limbs, at a distance of forty or fifty feet, the loop of an ordinary rope. He is also an expert in riding and training refractory horses and mules. A stubborn horse belonging to one of our butchers was persuaded to bear him gently on its back, and follow him about the streets. On Saturday, Dave Brock declared that one of his mules, then hitched to wagon, could not be ridden by anybody. This caused a smile to play upon the countenance of the young Mexican, who declared that he would ride any mule on the planet, including Brock's, for five dollars. But Dave didn't want to risk more than a dollar. By this time, a blind man with an organ had drawn a crowd about the east side of the square, the Mexican assisting by rattling the bones. The blind man sought a collection, but a number of those in the crowd wanted to see the mule throw the Mexican, and took up a counter collection, beating the blind man badly, raising three dollars, which was offered to the rattler of bones, if he would ride Dave's mule. He consented, a saddle was procured, and the two hundred people left the blind man in his glory and proceeded to the grounds just southwest of the old fair ground, wither had gone the mule and the Mexican. Here matters were soon arranged, and during the utmost curiosity of the crowd, the man mounted the animal. And such "bucking," rearing, and bounding no other mule ever went through with, the rider clinging to his back, laughing and waving his hat. Soon the mule found that he was mastered and trotted away as gently as a cow. The performance lasted ten minutes, and a more perfect reformation of mule stubbornness was never accomplished. Dismounting, our Mexican friend received his three dollars and strolled. But a number thought the mule might change its mind, and insisted that he should ride again. Accordingly he mounted the second time, and the animal moved as steadily as the best trained horse. After going about one hundred yards, direction was changed, and the rider "let the mule out." It came toward the crowd, and halted as orderly as possible when the rider drew the reins. The reformation was complete. Dave Brock had been thrown by the animal "higher than a kite," although Dave counts himself a good rider. And now a countryman rode it to the hitching rack without trouble. This Mexican is a handy man to have around.

The story continued in the *Ledger* of June 8: "The Mexican, trainer of fractious animals and festive lariat slinger, has donned the garb of an Indian and plays his part with amazing aptness."

More was reported in the *Ledger* of June 15:

John, the Mexican, again distinguished himself on Tuesday as a rider. An immense mule belonging to a young countryman with a black velvet coat was said to be very remarkable for jumping stiff legged and landing riders over his head; especially so if anything that rattled was carried by the person on his back. John was challenged and accepted a proposition to ride for a reasonable collection; the inconsiderable sum of $1.25 was contributed by the crowd of two or three hundred people, and the intrepid Mexican mounted, armed with a string of sleigh bells and heavily spurred. The first clatter of bells sent the mule and the rider into the air; and thus for fifteen minutes the animal cavorted about the corner of Conner Street *and the railroad, the rider clinging to his back in fine style, laughing, shouting, ringing the bells, and planting his spurs into the sides of the haughty mule. The cavorting was continued by the addition of a dollar to the collection. The show was equal to a circus, and during all of it, the Mexican maintained his reputation for staying with mule flesh.*

This quote from the *Anderson Herald* about a Sunday school excursion to Noblesville appeared in the *Ledger* on June 22:

"Mexican John," a Spanish halfbreed, who has been electrifying Noblesville for some time past with his wonderful proficiency in throwing the lasso, accompanied the excursion and afforded unbounded amusement to a large crowd of small boys, as well as those of larger growth, by exhibitions of his dexterity. "Mexican John" desires us to announce that in a few weeks he contemplates visiting Anderson, when he will take pleasure in riding any or all unmanageable colts, mules, or donkeys that may be brought him.

There is no record of the man after this time. It would be interesting to learn what brought him from Mexico to Noblesville in the 1870s.

The First Chinese Immigrants

While Hamilton County has people of many different nationalities living here today, at one time it was rare enough to be reported in the news. The *Ledger* reported on December 14, 1883, that "a Chinaman, the first on record, was in town Monday." The man may have been looking at commercial properties because the first Chinese laundry in the county was opened in August 1884. It was operated by a man named Sam Hing. By December, Hing had closed the business because of personal health issues. The paper said that he had been a good workman.[91]

On July 8, 1887, a new Chinese laundry was opened by a man named Tie Loy. Loy would live in Noblesville for several years and became a well-known member of the community. His background is uncertain. The 1900 census said he was born in 1848 and had immigrated in 1883. His arrival may have been earlier since it was later noted that he was a naturalized citizen and could vote. The Chinese Exclusion Act had been passed in 1882, which prevented Chinese people from immigrating or becoming citizens.[92]

Loy sold the laundry to a man named Yee Wah in April 1888 and moved to Bloomington for a short time. Wah ran the business from April to July. Then, from October 1888 to March 1889, the Noblesville Laundry (which may or may not have been the same business) was run by men named Lee Wah and Pong Hi. Loy had returned to Noblesville by January 1890, when he gave some Chinese plums to a *Ledger* reporter who had never seen them.[93]

In 1891, a steam laundry was built to compete with Loy's business. It failed and was purchased by Loy in 1892. Loy was very involved with the community, for example, donating twenty dollars to the construction of the Presbyterian church in 1893. In 1894, he married twenty-four-year-old Lydia J. Kilde, whose parents were immigrants from Ireland. He was listed as Chan Tie Loy in the marriage record, which is the only place this appears. His first child, a boy named Frank, was born in November 1895. The marriage was not always a happy one; there are reports in the newspaper of severe arguments.[94]

Loy was interested in politics, and when a big Republican rally was held in 1896, he furnished material to make souvenirs. He would continue to vote in elections up to 1902. He took his young son to see the visit of President William McKinley in October 1898. At one point, he held the boy high enough to see inside the president's railroad car, where Mrs. McKinley saw him and smiled at him.[95]

Sadly, the child died in November 1898 of Bright's disease and was buried in Crownland Cemetery. The newspaper said the boy was a favorite of people along Eighth Street and "the humble couple have the sympathy of the entire community." Loy's wife had been pregnant when the boy died, and in January 1899, the paper reported, "Tie Loy, the Chinese laundryman, and his American wife are the proud possessors of a new born girl baby." The daughter was named Ethel M. Loy.[96]

In April 1899, Loy went to Cicero to buy equipment from another Chinese laundry after the death of its owner, Sam Kee, whom the paper called "an old acquaintance" of Loy's. Kee's son Pang came from California to settle things. Tie Loy opened a laundry in Arcadia in July 1900 and moved his family there.[97]

There was an interesting story that appeared in the *Ledger* in July of that year. They had noticed that on Memorial Day, Loy had gone to the burial site of his son in Crownland Cemetery and placed bananas, candy, eggs and other things on the grave. Unfortunately, the story was part of an article called "Chinese Character" that made sneering comments about "superstitions" and "these slow plodding people."[98]

In August, it was reported in the Arcadia newspaper that the family was suffering from extreme poverty. It also mentioned that his wife, Lydia, had epilepsy. While people from town gave provisions and money, prejudice was becoming more obvious. The article concluded with the line "It would not look well for even a 'heathen Chinee' to starve to death in Arcadia."[99]

The family moved to the county poor farm in September 1901. The newspaper reported that a child of Loy's, probably the daughter, died in January 1902, and this child was also buried in Crownland Cemetery. Apparently, neither grave is marked with a headstone.[100]

There were stories of possible abuse at the county home, including Lydia being beaten. Loy got out and attempted to revive his business in 1903. However, he was losing his eyesight and was unable to work. His wife divorced him that year and would remarry in 1905.[101]

Loy moved to Indianapolis in 1904. The last reports of him are garbled. For some reason, the newspapers confused him with a man named Chan Yin Sun. Both men were determined to return to China to die and be buried in their homeland. Tie Loy left the United States by March 1904.[102]

Self-Emancipation

John Burtwell

Westfield was an important stop in Indiana for the Underground Railroad, and the stories of the fugitives who came through town are still being discovered. One of the notable ones was escaped slave, barber and politician John Burtwell, a noted person in his day.

Since Burtwell began his life in slavery in the Deep South, information is very difficult to find prior to his arrival in Hamilton County. The information that exists comes from census records, his death record and various newspaper articles (many of which have errors). He was born in Alabama to a woman named Keziah. She was owned by the Bedford family, while John and his father, Andrew, were owned by the Burtwell family of Florence, Alabama. The slave owner, John Trumball Burtwell, was a steamboat captain whose wife was a member of the Bedford family.[103]

According to later newspaper accounts, John became a cook aboard Burtwell's boat. Sometime in the 1850s, it docked at Lawrenceburg, Indiana, and John was sent ashore on an errand. He took the opportunity to escape. He found members of the Underground Railroad who pointed him toward Westfield. He was there by 1860, when he was listed in the census record as living with and working for Levi and Hannah Bowman. The accounts state that the slave owner later came to Westfield to look for John but was discouraged by the locals.[104]

As was common for slaves, John's birthdate is unknown, even the year. The 1860 census says that he was 35 years old, while the 1880 census says that he was 49. The 1900 and 1910 censuses follow this pattern, and his

1911 death record says that he was 102. The newspaper accounts put his age even higher and claim that he was 110 in 1906 or 112 in 1911. They also say his mother lived to the age of 125. While these ages are very unlikely, the alleged longevity did mean that his story was of interest and got recorded.[105]

A significant part of his story (which was forgotten later) happened in 1864. John ran in the election for township trustee of Washington Township, making him the first African American to run for office in Hamilton County. What is more significant is that in the Westfield precinct, he placed second out of a field of three. The totals were George Catterson, 100; John Burtwell, 48; and Jesse Sparks, 46.

We know about this because of an irate editorial that appeared in the *Indianapolis Star* (which was unconnected to today's *Indianapolis Star*) in April of that year. Titled "Miscegenation," it dismissed Burtwell as "contraband from the south." It went on to say, "The fellows who voted for Burtwell may think the white man as good as the negro if he behaves himself, but their votes show that they place the African above their own race."[106]

John doesn't appear in the 1870 census, possibly because he was away from the state. Many former slaves spent time after the Civil War searching through the South for lost family members. He was apparently successful because there was an African American woman in Hamilton County named Sarah Burtwell who married Charles S. Morgan in 1876. Sarah S. Morgan was the person who signed Burtwell's death certificate.[107]

In the 1880 census, the Burtwell household consists of Keziah Bedford (age seventy-four), her son John Burtwell (age forty-nine) and her grandson Luther B. Burtwell (age eight). John is listed as an agricultural laborer, but the Helms 1880 history says that he is a barber. According to the 1900 census, he was living by himself, employed as a day laborer and was unable to read or write. Despite being illiterate, he owned property in Westfield, including his own house, which in 1910 was on Penn Street.

There is no record of Luther Burtwell after 1880. Sarah S. Morgan lived in Lafayette, Indiana. The newspaper accounts say that John's mother lived with him until she died, but there is no record of when that happened. In May 1911, John's house burned, and he had to move to the county home in Noblesville.[108] Evidently, the stress of events proved too difficult for him, and he died on June 6. The death record says that he was buried in Summit Lawn Cemetery in Westfield, but there is apparently no headstone.

An Early African American Political Statement

There is a photo that shows an interesting incident in Noblesville's political history. The background on it is from an undated article in the Hamilton East Public Library collection published sometime around 1910–22, probably in the *Noblesville Times* and titled "Noblesville Holds First Negro Grant and Wilson Pole Raising." The photo was owned by an African American resident of Noblesville named Belle Bush (1858–1926) and shows the southeast corner of Courthouse Square at the intersection of Ninth and Conner Streets. Only one of the buildings in the picture is still there.

This was a political rally on August 8, 1872, to support the election of Ulysses S. Grant. A pole raising was a community building activity and an act dating back to classical Rome meant to symbolize the overthrow of tyranny. The pole was particularly significant in this case because the rally was organized by the African American community of central Indiana. The Fifteenth Amendment to the Constitution had been passed in 1870, giving citizens the right to vote, no matter their "race, color, or condition of previous servitude," and this was the first presidential election in which many African Americans were able to vote.

The 1872 election pitted Grant and Henry Wilson (Republican) against a collection of other candidates, such as Horace Greeley (Liberal Republican), Thomas Hendricks of Indiana (Democrat) and Victoria Woodhull (Equal Rights Party)—the first woman ever to run for president.

African American pole raising at a rally for Ulysses S. Grant, corner of Ninth and Conner Streets, 1872. *Dana Hughes collection.*

The newspaper article said about the event in Noblesville:

> *Reports of the day state that there were thousands of colored people in Noblesville for the celebration. Special trains were run from Indianapolis and a colored military company from Indianapolis, known as Grants Military Guards was present in a body to do the honors of the day.*
>
> *The pole was 160 feet long and was equipped with a mammoth Grant and Wilson flag. Cannons were fired with the final bringing of the pole into position, and the military companies' salute is said to have reverberated up and down the White River Valley.*

Some of the men involved in raising the pole were identified as Aaron Mitchell, Clark "Major" Howard, Rick Munden, Henry Johnson, Greenberry Roper, Albert Wallace and Henry Hedgpath.

Later that day, a barbecue was held at the county fairgrounds (now the site of North Elementary School), where speeches were given and the program continued. The keynote speaker was to have been Hiram R. Revels, the first African American elected to the U.S. Senate.

Unfortunately, Revels missed the train out of Indianapolis and was unable to be present. Local speakers were found instead, and Lin Carlin's Silver Cornet Band and the Westfield band furnished the music during the day. Among other things, the barbecue raised funds for the construction of a building for the First Baptist Church. Today, that building is the Birdie Gallery of the Hamilton County Artists Association.

While the raising of poles at political rallies was not unusual at this time, this allegedly was the first one in the United States organized by African Americans. Since many of them had recently been freed from slavery before moving to Indiana, this adds a special significance.

STEPHEN ROBERTS

Another Sort of Stockbroker

Stephen "Steve" Roberts was born in Roberts Settlement to Stephen and Mary Roberts. His grandfather Willis had been one of the first emigrants to the settlement in the 1830s. Sources differ on the younger Stephen's birthdate, but the 1900 census says that he was born in March 1848. Stephen was one of several children—his older brother Junius served in the Civil War in the Twenty-Eighth United States Colored Troops—and he was only outlived by three of his sisters: Martha, Jennie and Anna.

He started out in life as a farmer like his father, but soon after the Civil War, he began working with white businessmen like Samuel Craig, Marion Aldred and others as a livestock buyer and shipper. Craig was a farmer and stock dealer, while Aldred eventually became a banker. Neither had problems working with an African American since Craig's father was an abolitionist minister and Aldred had been a soldier in the Union army.[109]

Stephen's business materials would be donated to the Library of Congress after his death, and the collection gives an idea of how his business was conducted. Among the materials are receipts for the "new" Exchange Stockyards and Manufacturing Company built in 1875 on south Kentucky Avenue in Indianapolis. This company eventually became the Union Stockyards and was one of the key businesses on the Belt Railroad that went around the city. (Today, the site is part of the Lilly campus.)

The animals would be purchased from the farmers; put on the Indianapolis, Peru and Chicago Railroad (which was the only railroad in Hamilton County in the 1870s); and sent to Indianapolis and then points east. Roberts's job gave him the opportunity to travel. Among the items in

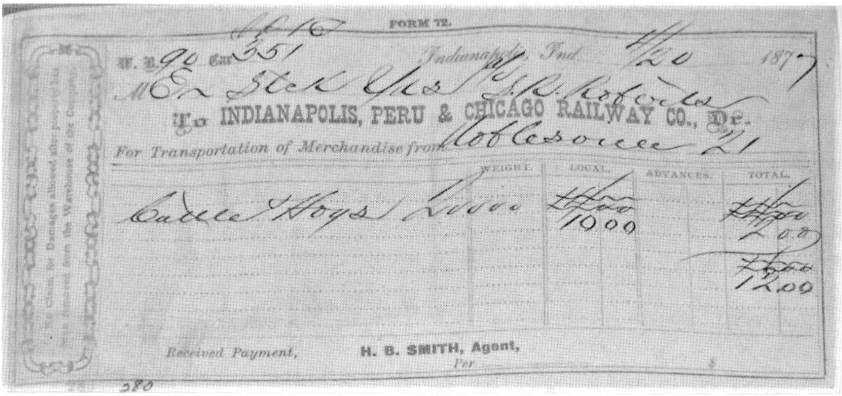
FORM 72.
Indianapolis, Ind. 1877
To INDIANAPOLIS, PERU & CHICAGO RAILWAY CO., Dr.
For Transportation of Merchandise from
WEIGHT. | LOCAL. | ADVANCES. | TOTAL.
Received Payment, H. B. SMITH, Agent, Per

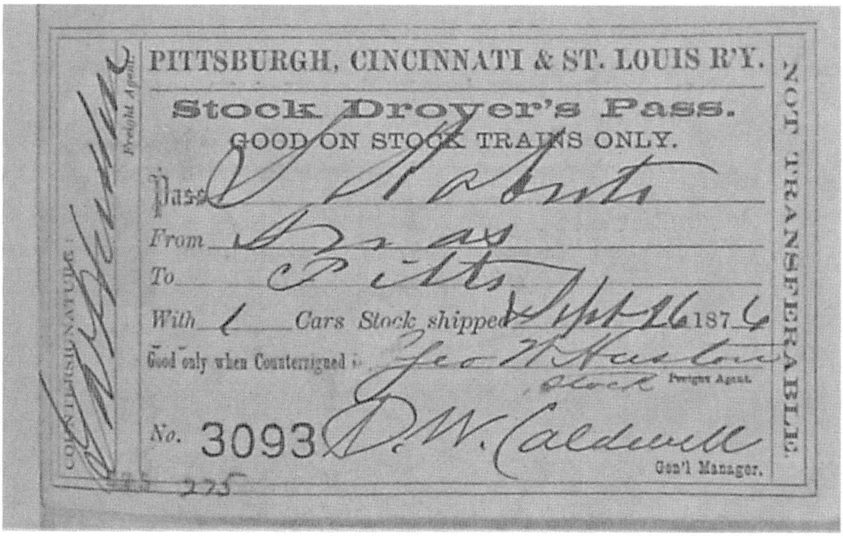
PITTSBURGH, CINCINNATI & ST. LOUIS R'Y.
Stock Drover's Pass.
GOOD ON STOCK TRAINS ONLY.
Pass
From
To
With Cars Stock shipped 187
Good only when Countersigned
Freight Agent.
No. 3093
Gen'l Manager.
NOT TRANSFERABLE.
COUNTERSIGNATURE.
Freight Agent.

Top: Receipt signed by Stephen Roberts, 1877. *Roberts Settlement collection, National Archives.*

Bottom: Railroad pass for Stephen Roberts, 1876. *Roberts Settlement collection, National Archives.*

the collection is a drover's pass to accompany a shipment of livestock on the railroad to Pittsburgh.

Stephen had moved to Noblesville by 1880 and married Nancy Eliot that year. She was born sometime around 1852 and was the first African American child born in Noblesville. They had two children: James, who died young, and Leroy or Roy. Roberts was described in one newspaper article as a big man with a powerful physique, and while he had a fine, friendly disposition, he was also "a man among men." This is illustrated by a

Noblesville 1890s baseball team; Leroy "Frosty" Roberts is in back, second from right. *Hamilton County Historical Society.*

newspaper story from 1882 that said that after a drunk had insulted Nancy, Stephen gave him what the paper called a "sound trouncing."[110]

His wife continued to work outside the home after the marriage and did what we would now refer to as catering. She organized and cooked food for the finest weddings in the area in the 1880s and 1890s, put on by the community's wealthiest citizens. She eventually became known as "Aunt Nan" and was as well respected by the people of Noblesville as her husband was by the farmers in the county.[111]

Their son Leroy held a variety of jobs, played on the town baseball team in the 1890s and was nicknamed "Frosty" by his friends. He was married in 1897 and had one daughter. However, he had a run of poor luck. In 1902, he lost part of his foot when he slipped under the wheels while he was trying to board a train. Later, he contracted some sort of throat trouble, which led to his death in 1924.[112]

Stephen died in 1915 and was buried at Crownland Cemetery. His son followed him in 1924. However, his wife lived on for many years, with the town putting on celebrations for her 90th and 99th birthdays. She died two weeks after her 100th birthday in 1952 and was buried alongside her husband and son.[113]

The Hord Brothers

Another notable African American family was the Hord or Hoard family, particularly three brothers: George (1838–1871), William (1844–1882) and John (1846–1884). When the Civil War started and Blacks were allowed to enlist, the brothers joined up. In 1863, William enlisted in the Fifty-Fifth Massachusetts Infantry—the companion regiment to the Fifty-Fourth, which was portrayed in the movie *Glory*. He served in South Carolina and was discharged for disability in 1865. John joined the Eighth United States Colored Infantry in January 1865, and George joined the same regiment in March. The Eighth served in Virginia and was one of the regiments present when Lee surrendered to Grant at Appomattox in April.[114]

George returned to Noblesville after the war, became a brakeman for the railroad and died in an accident in 1871. William stayed in South Carolina, and during the Reconstruction era, he was able to become a member of the Charleston Police Department as a detective, serving between 1869 and 1874. However, he was discharged from the force and served time in jail after illegally shooting at someone.[115]

John had returned to Noblesville as well. He was the one who took the radical step of running for city constable in the 1880 election. As shown elsewhere in this book, Black law enforcement officers were not unprecedented in Hamilton County.

The year 1880 seemed to be a good one politically for Hamilton County African Americans. Eli Roberts was running for county recorder, Green

Grave of John Hoard with the wrong inscription, Riverside Cemetery. *Bryan Glover photo.*

Roper Sr. was appointed to the county petit jury and Frederick Douglass came to town to speak for the national ticket.[116]

John won the election handily, and the newspaper reported it as: "John Hoard, the colored man, who was a candidate on the Republican township ticket for constable of Noblesville, was elected by the handsome majority of one hundred and six over the democratic candidate. 'Rah for John. Blood will tell."[117]

Many of the people who voted for him had also been veterans of the war, and their attitudes had a big influence on the town at the time. He was only able to serve for four years before he died of consumption. He had been a member of the local branch of the veterans' organization, the Grand Army of the Republic, and they put a memorial in the paper that read, in part:

> *Whereas, resolved, that in his death, this post has lost a faithful comrade, his wife and children a devoted husband and protector, and the community a good citizen;*
>
> *Resolved, that his wife and child have our sincere condolence and sympathy in their sad bereavement;*
>
> *Resolved, that our late comrade, John Hord, with others that have fallen shall be remembered by us in the decoration of their graves on each succeeding 30th of May.*[118]

Ironically, the newspaper notice lists the wrong regiment for him, which is compounded by the fact that his gravestone is also marked with the wrong regiment. The newspaper says "28th USCT," and his gravestone says "54th Massachusetts." His brother George is buried nearby and has "28th USCT" marked on his stone. The errors are unfortunate, but African American participation in the war was being forgotten, and it was good that the local people thought enough of him to remember him.

The brothers actually have another memorial today. The City of Noblesville has recognized them by naming a street at Hamilton Town Center "Hoard Drive."

Charles Dempsey

Buffalo Soldier

Possibly the only soldier from Hamilton County to have seen combat during the Spanish-American War was Charles A. Dempsey. Evidently, military service ran in the family, because Charles's father, George, served in the Civil War as part of the Twenty-Eighth U.S. Colored Troops.

George, who was born in Indiana in 1845, enlisted on February 5, 1864, and service records show that he was entitled to a $300 bounty. He spent the early part of his term in the hospital. The records say that it had to do with an "irritable stomach" and was serious enough that he was sent to a large hospital in Pennsylvania. He returned to duty on September 18, 1864, and was assigned guard duty at a prisoner of war camp at Point Lookout, Maryland. He was discharged from the army on November 8, 1865, and returned to Noblesville. When a reunion of his regiment was held in Indianapolis in 1895, he was elected president of the organization. He died in 1935.[119]

George married Nancy Winslow on February 24, 1867. Their first son, Frank, was born in 1868 and Charles was born on his parents' anniversary in 1869. A sister named Mamie was born in 1871. George later left the family, taking Mamie with him, and had remarried by 1878. Frank and Charles were raised by their mother. Interestingly, the Hamilton East Public Library has its circulation record from the 1880s, and there are a number of library visits by "C. Dempsey" and "F. Dempsey"—very likely the two brothers. They checked out books on a variety of subjects.[120]

Spanish-American War soldiers at state fairgrounds. *Earl Brooks Collection, Hamilton County Historical Society.*

Charles first enlisted in the army at Cincinnati on November 9, 1887. He was assigned to the Tenth Cavalry, which was known as the "Buffalo Soldiers." Unfortunately, there are no records of his service. He was discharged as a private on February 19, 1890, in San Carlos, Arizona Territory. He came back to Noblesville and married Ruth Freeman on November 27, 1890.[121]

When the Spanish-American War threatened, he reenlisted in Indianapolis on May 9, 1898, and was assigned to the Twenty-Fourth Infantry, Company G. Again, there are no records of his service, but later newspaper accounts said that he was part of the Battle of El Caney and the siege at Santiago from July 1 to July 4. The Twenty-Fourth Infantry was an important part of the famous charge up San Juan Hill, but there are no records that show his participation. He was back in Noblesville on September 30 for a city celebration of the soldiers at the county courthouse courtroom. The large crowd made several calls for him to speak since he was the only county resident to see action. He was discharged from the army on January 27, 1899, as a private with a good record. A February 3 newspaper reported that he needed a cane to walk because of rheumatism contracted in the trenches at Santiago, but the condition was getting better.[122]

Spanish-American War soldiers at state fairgrounds. *Earl Brooks Collection, Hamilton County Historical Society.*

Ruth Dempsey died on April 21, 1900, after an eight-month illness, and Charles married Elizabeth Spinks on December 20, 1900. He became involved in community activities. He began preaching at the First Baptist Church in March 1903 and was awarded an army pension in August of that year. However, racial tensions may have been growing. He took a political stand in 1904 when he wrote a letter to the *Indianapolis Recorder* newspaper on March 12. He talked about how Black men like Levi Scott, Reverend John Burden and Fred J. Hord were being turned down and forced off the county election board. This may have been the reason that he moved to Chicago, where he is listed in the 1910 census.[123]

In the 1920 census, he was living in Los Angeles, California, and working as a bricklayer. He applied to live in a soldiers' home due to his many physical problems but was still listed as living at home in the 1930 census. He died on December 9, 1955, and was buried at Fort Gibson National Cemetery in Oklahoma.[124]

A Secret Hate Group

The Junior Order of United American Mechanics

While talking about notable Hamilton County African Americans is important, it needs to be remembered that there were serious problems in the county through the years. The Ku Klux Klan is the most well known of the hate groups, but there were others that appeared.

The Order of United American Mechanics was a nativist, anti-Catholic group that was formed in Pennsylvania in the 1840s as a reaction to German and Irish immigration. Descriptions of it first appeared in Indiana newspapers in 1849. The group used Masonic symbols, but there was no official connection to the Freemasons. A youth group was formed in 1853 that was called the "Junior Order." Members of the original group were called the "Senior Order." After some later reorganizations, the youth group became the primary group.[125]

There was an attempt to organize a Hamilton County chapter in 1876, led by Noblesville bookseller Arza Truitt, which had no success.[126] Catholic immigrants had come into the county thirty to forty years before with the Mullen and Buscher Settlements and were now considered part of the community. This attitude changed after the failure of the 1887 gas boom.

A Hamilton County chapter of the Junior Order of United American Mechanics (JOUAM) was organized in December 1901. It was called "Hamilton Council No. 8." The national JOUAM had a women's auxiliary group called the Daughters of Liberty that was started in 1875. A Hamilton County women's auxiliary group called the Daughters of America was formed in December 1905.[127]

Official insignia of the Junior Order of United American Mechanics. *Detail from an image in* Official History of the Junior Order United American Mechanics, *edited by Edw. S. Deemer, 1897.*

Members of the organization made strong political statements in the newspapers as they approached their fifth anniversary in 1906. They made it very clear that their focus was restriction of immigration. They said that they were concerned about health issues, pauper issues and, most importantly, competition for jobs with native-born workers. One quote said that if the then-present rate of immigration continued, in one hundred years, native-born workers would be as "extinct as the moundbuilders." The statewide meeting was held in Noblesville in October.[128]

However, as time went along, the political side of the Hamilton County JOUAM seemed to fade. They gave the appearance of a typical fraternal social/insurance organization, like the Oddfellows, the Woodmen of the World and the Knights of Pythias. Mentions in the newspaper through the 1910s were mostly about social events and meetings, with no public political statements. Then, as the Ku Klux Klan became more prominent after World War I, the local JOUAM disappeared almost completely.[129]

The rise of the Klan made the JOUAM politically redundant. Along with race, the KKK had made its animosity clear about immigrants and Catholics, up to the point of a clash with the Notre Dame football team. African American author Cyrus Colter was born in Noblesville in 1910 and spent the first years of his life here. In later years, he remembered actually witnessing a KKK meeting sometime around 1916. He said most of what he heard were anti-Catholic statements.[130]

The Indiana Klan collapsed after the D.C. Stephenson trial in 1925. In August, in the midst of the trial, records for the local Klavern were dumped in White River. The local group continued with a lower profile through 1926, with the Ladies of the Klan celebrating their second anniversary in February. However, there was outrage when Stephenson opened his records and the group's political and financial scandals became public. By 1927, politicians all over the state were being indicted for their corrupt connections or distancing themselves from the organization. The state attorney general spent much of 1928 trying to get the state organization's charter revoked.

This makes it significant that there was a big revival of the Noblesville JOUAM in March 1927. There were large recruiting notices in the newspaper and articles about the great number of new candidates being initiated. Interestingly, the group met at the same site that the Klan had met before its collapse: the Red Men's Lodge at Tenth and Logan Streets.[131]

More importantly, there was a witness to this revival. In the book *Rail Fences, Rolling Pins, and Rainbows*, there is a chapter about the reminiscences of a man named Larry Venable when he was a young boy in Noblesville in the 1920s. Among other things, he openly declares that the local KKK took over the JOUAM. He says that his father, William E. Venable, belonged to the group. In fact, according to newspaper accounts, his father was one of the officers of the group.[132]

Venable states that the group was doing many of the same rituals and using the same regalia as the Klan, including burning crosses. There was a small electrically powered cross that was used at the meeting. Larry was a good singer, and he said that he was expected to join in on songs like "The Old Fiery Cross." When the group put together a minstrel show in 1931, Larry was pushed to be a performer. In the account and in later discussions with his family, he clearly expressed his dislike for being forced to participate in the group.

The only public political statement from this time period that can be found is a listing of the group's objectives, which were aimed at "native-born Americans." The first objective was to "promote the interests of Americans and to shield them from the depressing effects of unrestricted immigration." Second was the creation of a benefits fund for members, third was to uphold free public schools and encourage the reading of the Bible in them, and fourth was to promote a national orphans' home. It was stated that there were other objectives, but they were not listed. Membership was for white males between sixteen and fifty-five who believed in God and were "in favor of free education, opposed to any union of Church and State, and to interference of any foreign power, directly or indirectly, with the government."[133]

The JOUAM was not a secret society like the Klan, so there are lists of members' names in the newspaper. It would be interesting to compare these lists to the known Klan list. Other than this, mentions in the papers were just notices for regular meetings and social events. This continued through the early 1930s, and then there was an urgent meeting called in March 1935. After this, the group disappeared from the newspaper. Any mention of the organization usually referred to the Elwood chapter, which was still going. Possibly the chapters had combined due to the pressures of the Great Depression. The JOUAM continued in other cities in central Indiana, with the Muncie group lasting until the mid-1970s.[134]

Part IV

LAW AND ORDER

The Battle of Tappin's Woodpile

In September 1864, there was an attempt to hold a Democrat or pro-Confederate political rally at the Hamilton County Fairgrounds on the north side of Noblesville. The local citizens objected strongly to this; there had been fights with "butternuts" before this. A Methodist minister named Safety Layton made a speech by a woodpile in front of Thomas Tappin's photography studio on Conner Street to counter it. The rallygoers objected to that, and arguments ensued, eventually becoming violent. A man named Pfaff was shot in the neck by a man named Trittipo, Trittipo's horse was killed, several leading citizens had to flee for their lives and the bell was rung in the courthouse to call up the militia. In later years, local people would nickname it "The Battle of Tappin's Woodpile."[135]

John Rhodes and the Sheriff's Posse

Hamilton County has several provable stories of the Underground Railroad, the most notable being that of John and Louann Rhodes. They arrived in the area in 1837 and fought a court case for their freedom in 1844. That story has been told elsewhere. However, it has an interesting sequel involving their son that is less well-known.

After their trial, the couple settled down in Hamilton County. The next year, 1845, their only son, John, was born. They eventually had five children and bought land to live on. When John Rhodes wrote his will in 1850, it was mostly straightforward legal terms to make sure his wife and children got everything. However, between the time that he wrote his will and the time he died, he added a marginal comment that showed he had not let his guard down. Separate from the main text, he wrote, "After my departure, I give to my son John Rhodes, one gun and one horse." It's not known exactly when he died, but the will was probated in January 1857. He was probably in his sixties.[136]

Louann may have died soon after that. The census record for 1860 shows the son, John, and the other children living with their older sister Lydia. By then, she had married a man named Charles Allen. Information in this period is very sketchy. The census record for 1870 shows no members of the family left in Hamilton County except for John. At that time, he was a farmhand for Jesse Baker. However, soon after this, he made a dramatic reappearance in the historic record.

Hamilton County sheriff's residence and jail, circa 1895. Sheriff Franklin Thacker with family and friends. Donated to HCHS by Susan Lucas, great-great-granddaughter of Sheriff Thacker. *Hamilton County Historical Society.*

He made this appearance because of the nature of Adams Township at this time. It was not as well settled as other parts of the county and was apparently something of a trouble area. The largest town was Boxley. The railroad had not come through, so Sheridan was just a little crossroads called Millwood. The impression given by the county newspaper of the time, the *Hamilton County Register*, is that church meetings were about the only social activity other than drinking. Of course, the drunks found it very entertaining to disrupt the church meetings, including shooting through the windows. Apparently, there were a few people who made a habit of it. The Harbaugh boys, Frank and Cass, were the leaders of such a group. The Harbaugh gang was also noted for committing robberies.

They met their match in the sheriff at that time, David W. Patty. He had come from a family of gunsmiths, served in the cavalry during the Civil War, been captured and spent time at Andersonville and was now reading to become a lawyer. He was almost overqualified for police work in the 1870s.[137] This is how the *Noblesville Register* of February 15, 1871, reported one of the confrontations between the Harbaughs and Patty:

> *Last Saturday night Sheriff Patty and Deputies Austin and Waddel visited the church called Phillippi four miles northwest of Cicero for the purpose of making a couple of arrests. The gentlemen who were wanted were Mr. Harbaugh and Mr. Bennett, the first on a charge of robbery, the latter for disturbing a meeting. They had been eluding the officers for some time and had talked of shooting and other foolishness. The Sheriff and his deputies walked in quietly and the Sheriff invited the preacher to stop his discourse for a minute or two, he then told the congregation to remain quiet and keep seated, that he had a warrant for a couple of young men and should arrest them. Mr. H. and Mr. B were soon ornamented with bracelets, the latter making some resistance. The Sheriff then said that if there was anyone who would go their bail, he would wait, but if not he would travel. One gentleman thought it rather rough to take the young men off so suddenly, but declined the Sheriff's polite invitation to bail them. The Sheriff and his party walked their prisoners a mile or so to where the horses were left, he there hired a wagon to take them to town, and in due time they were put in a place where there was no danger of their getting hurt, the next day some of their friends bailed them out.*

However, the sheriff had some problems the next time he was in the area, according to the *Register* of March 8: "Sheriff Patty met with a serious accident last Friday. He was up near Boxley on business, his horse fell on him putting his arm out of place. He was brought down on Saturday, and is doing duty in Court this week. These old soldiers take a terrible sight of killing."

So, with the sheriff out of commission, the only way to deal with the Harbaugh gang was to form a group of special deputies—what in other circumstances might be called a "posse." One member of the group, and probably the first person whom Patty chose, was Dr. Cyrus Burrows, the town doctor of Boxley. Three other local men were also asked to join, but details about them are not clear.

The last two posse members are the only ones besides Burrows that are certain. One was Henry White, a Black twenty-three-year-old man, unmarried, and whose father, Dennison White, was one of the early settlers of Roberts's Settlement.[138] The other was John Rhodes.

Why did Rhodes and White become involved? It is not known what their motivation was. It may have been simply a sense of civic duty or a personal reason. Whatever their reason, it was obvious from the news story that they were effective. (Incidentally, the newspaper uses various slang terms, some of which are inappropriate today, to describe the African American members of the party.) The phrase "Fifteenth Amendments" in this excerpt from the *Register* on March 15, 1871, was a reference to the newly passed amendment to the Constitution giving the right of citizenship to former slaves.

> Column 3: *"On Monday night a party composed partly of Fifteenth Amendments, made a raid in Adams township capturing Cass Harbaugh and Frank Harbaugh, at the residence of Daniel Lane, five miles northwest of Boxley; they also captured Lemuel Haines at the residence of Vic Haines. These are the gentlemen who have been eluding the Sheriff for some time. There were six persons in the party which captured them—they were John Rhodes, Henry White, W.D. Horney, A. Smith, J. Elliot, and Burrows. The three men who were wanted are now in jail awaiting further proceedings."*
>
> Column 1: *"The Harbaugh boys and Lew Haines have come to grief. They were taken up by a party of the Fifteenth Amendment. They say they would not have cared so much to be taken if the d-----d* [n-----s] *had not done it."*
>
> Column 2: *"Circuit Court Case of the State vs. Harbaugh was nolie pros'd and the defendant gave security for his appearance to answer any indictment that may be found."*

So, the Harbaugh boys were out of jail on bail again. This was obviously too much for one of the residents of Boxley, who then wrote a letter to the *Register* on March 22:

> *Sir—For some time our Sheriff, Mr. Patty, has been operating in this section of the country trying to catch a certain gang of desperados, by name Cass*

> *Harbaugh, Frank Harbaugh, and Lemuel Hains. But not being successful he deputized Dr. C. Burrows for that business, and he in company with Messrs. Harvey, Elliot, Smith, Roads, and White, the last two being colored gentlemen, made the arrest, and on Tuesday morning safely landed them in jail. But this morning (Wednesday), they are back again, with the report that they were acquitted. Now the question is, is this so? If it is, where is the justice in the law? These men were arrested for theft, all of them, under the most aggravating circumstances. Was it because there was no evidence? Surely not, for there is enough of evidence against them to send them to the penitentiary. Was it because of any deficiency on the part of the prosecuting attorney? It surely was not that, for the county pays enough to secure the best talent. Then, why was it? How does it come that desperados cannot have justice meted out to them? How long must a civil community suffer? If this was the first time, we could excuse it, but it is not by many. Our religious exercises are disturbed night after night by those same men and have we any assurance that they will atone of themselves?*

Unfortunately, on the microfilm, the rest of the letter is illegible, including the name. It is here that the historic record dries up. The next issues of the paper up to 1874 are missing. The materials at the county courthouse from this period are very sporadic.

As for John Rhodes, the rest of his family had already left the county. He and his sister Elizabeth sold the last of their father's land in 1873. Interestingly, the next time John appears, he is on the wrong side of the law. He was courting the sheriff's cook in May 1875 when the two went to a social event that turned into an altercation. It happened again in September when he was with a couple of friends. The newspaper called these altercations "bellings." The second time, John was brought before the judge and fined fifteen dollars. The newspaper, which described John as being physically big and handsome, said that the judge spoke to John and told him that he hoped that John would settle down and become an asset to the community. The impression is given that people in the community liked Rhodes when he wasn't being rambunctious.[139]

Unfortunately, it may never be known if John Rhodes settled down. There is no more mention of him after 1875, and he is not in the 1880 Hamilton County census. It is possible he moved out of the area to be with his family.

Temperance Stories

White Cappers

Westfield has become a very hip community in the twenty-first century, particularly with regard to alcohol. Brewpubs and taprooms have opened, and there is even a craft beer and music festival. This would be a shock to the original settlers of the town, who were strongly in favor of temperance. Today, the temperance movement has a humorous stereotype of hymn-singing women with occasional saloon-smashing hatchet wielders like Carrie Nation. In reality, violence was surprisingly common. In fact, there was a secret society to enforce morality—by any means possible. In the late nineteenth century, Hamilton County had to deal with the night-riding vigilante group known as the White Caps.

The roots of the organization are in 1830s Indiana, when it was created for extra-legal frontier justice. The group's primary goals were temperance and protecting women, and its members were named for wearing white hoods to disguise themselves. One of their trademark actions was to ride up to a house with an abusive husband, take him outside and flog him.

Temperance and reform took off in the 1870s and 1880s, both legally and illegally. It was reported in 1875 that a court charged six Hamilton County Quakers $200 apiece for burning down a house of prostitution. In 1878, a group of men attacked a saloon in Clarksville.[140]

The movement was partially spurred by growth in the area. The Midland Railroad made its way through the county in the 1870s and 1880s, and the

Monon Railroad was finished in 1882. Houses of prostitution grew up along the "wrong side of the tracks." The growth, and attendant vice, increased with the discovery of natural gas in 1887.

In February 1889, the Noblesville mayor denied that there were White Cappers in the area. As if in answer, in March a man was attacked in Sheridan for improper relations with a woman. There were two attributed attacks in 1891 in Noblesville: a beating with hoses filled with sawdust and a dunking in the river. A Fishers man claimed that he had been beaten by White Caps in 1892, but it turned out that his wife had done it to punish him for drinking.[141]

Despite all this, a couple of Broad Ripple men unwisely attempted to open a saloon in Westfield in 1893. No White Caps showed up, but the church bells were rung to call everyone into town. At first, there was a confrontation at the town council. When neither side backed down, the men from Broad Ripple were arrested and fined for carrying concealed weapons. The judge offered them choice of jail until they could pay the fine or remittance if they signed a document saying they would not open a saloon. One signed the document, and the other went to jail. The Westfield citizens then released a statement: "We respectfully warn all whom it may concern to desist from any such attempt; for, if persisted in, the will of the people will be enforced. Come what may, the people will not tolerate a saloon in this place."[142]

The story of the White Caps in Hamilton County took a particularly frightening turn in 1909 with the harassment of a Mexican family in Fall Creek Township. There was no visible connection to alcohol or abuse. Soon after this, the Ku Klux Klan reappeared in Indiana. The KKK, under the charismatic leadership of D.C. Stephenson, rebranded themselves as a new form of White Cappers during Prohibition and the perceived decadence of the Roaring Twenties. They claimed that they were keeping America strong and healthy and protecting American womanhood. This created a strange alliance of descendants of abolitionists and the KKK.[143] One of the reasons that the Klan collapsed when Stephenson was put on trial for murder is that he was exposed as a drunk and a rapist, negating their rebranding.

The state government had been trying to clamp down on the White Caps, and after the collapse of the Klan, the issue started to fade away. There were incidents of vigilantism and lynching in other Indiana counties, but Hamilton County settled down.

The Westfield Saloon

Anyone who wants to start a business knows that there are many steps to follow involving ordinances, inspections, licenses and so on. However, even if your paperwork is all in order, community opposition might have a big effect on your success. As a saloon owner found out in Westfield in 1882, it can have a direct physical impact on your business plans.

From the beginning of its existence, the town of Westfield did not have businesses that sold alcohol. The staunch Quaker citizens did not use them and openly discouraged any that may have been built within the city limits. However, in 1882, the Chicago, Indianapolis and Louisville Railroad (later called the Monon) was being finished. It would cross the Midland Railroad just outside the town of Westfield. This railroad crossroads would increase business and bring in a new kind of settler. In the summer of 1882, a man named William Shaw decided to take advantage of this new population and established a saloon. Many saloons at this time were rough board buildings where a plank across two barrels might serve as a bar counter. This is probably the sort of place that Shaw had, although he had gone to the trouble to get a proper liquor license from the government. The saloon was also built outside the city limits, which meant the city fathers were unable to take any sort of action. Therefore, the city mothers decided to take matters into their own hands.

The Quaker women of Westfield were always known for being strong-minded. They were leaders in the Hamilton County abolition movement, the Underground Railroad, women's rights and other social issues. When it came to temperance and prohibition of alcohol, their "intemperate" response to a saloon in their midst showed that they were willing to take physical action.

The saloon had not been open long when a group of women came to the door. According to the *Republican-Ledger* newspaper, they requested that the owner close up his shop and offered to buy out his stock. He refused, whereupon the women descended on the building, trashed it and dumped out all the liquor that was available. However, Shaw considered this a temporary setback and soon had the place rebuilt and restocked. Since the building was little more than a shanty, the cost of decorating was low. He continued on like this for about another month.[144]

Monday, August 14, was probably a fairly quiet day in Westfield—except for the forty women assembled at the Quaker meetinghouse. They had decided it was time to send a message. As soon as they were all assembled, they picked up their axes and marched west to the railroad right-of-way where the saloon had been built. There were both Quaker and Methodist women in the group. One eyewitness recalled how the drab gray and brown dresses of the Quaker women contrasted with the bright dress of the Methodist women. He also said the Quaker women were bareheaded, as the distinctive Quaker bonnet would only interfere with the action.[145]

As the women approached the site, a wagon was seen driving in the opposite direction as fast as it could go. Shaw had attempted to stalemate the protest by removing most of his stock to a safe place. He also stood guard. The women, however, were undaunted. (They were the wives of some of the most respected men in the county. Had anyone physically confronted them, the situation would have gotten much uglier.) They brushed past Shaw and set axe to wood. This time, they didn't go for half measures. In the space of a few minutes, the structure was completely demolished. The women then took some last liquor bottles, poured them over the pile of scraps and set fire to them. The building was soon reduced to a heap of smoking ashes. The women hoped that Shaw would take the hint.

After the fire had died down, Shaw wanted to make a deal. He would give up his license and leave town if he was paid for damages and for the rest of his stock. The women then convened a meeting, and twenty-five dollars was offered to him as payment. He was also to promise never to open a saloon again. It was an offer he couldn't refuse. The rest of the liquor was then brought back and poured into the creek. Before adjourning the meeting, the women passed a resolution that was printed in the local papers:

> *Whereas, we are informed that persons from a distance have asserted that they would set up saloons in Westfield, therefore,*
>
> *RESOLVED: That notice is hereby given that no saloons will be tolerated in our midst, and that all persons coming here to engage in the business will come at their peril.*
>
> *Mrs. M.H. Brown, President*

Sometime after this, Shaw was seen sporting a blue ribbon on his lapel. Since blue ribbons were the insignia of a temperance campaign started by Francis Murphy in the 1870s, somehow the incident had inspired him to take a pledge not to drink liquor.[146]

Westfield would not allow alcohol to be sold until the 1970s. By then, Hamilton County had become a very different sort of place. The site of Shaw's saloon was eventually occupied by the world's largest Dairy Queen. Although this kind of direct action is no longer condoned today, it put an interesting twist on the modern idea of community feedback.

The 1883 Newspaper War

Since the earliest days of journalism, newspapers have known that a way to attract readers is to find something sensational and create a news event. Other newspapers would then respond to create a media hullabaloo that was sometimes out of proportion to the original subject. In the early 1880s, the Noblesville papers evidently got tired of topics like the new telephone system and trotting races. The *Republican-Ledger* went all out in October 1883 and wrote a series of articles titled "Noblesville's Bagnios."

The articles allegedly exposed Noblesville's houses of ill repute. They went into extraordinary detail, which is helpful to historians but would be very legally questionable today. The articles were answered by the *Independent*, which said that they were based on unfounded rumor. The *Republican-Ledger* then accused the editor of the *Independent* of being a defender of houses of ill fame. It was a sordid topic, but the exchange of views was lively.

The articles list locations of the houses, names of the women, nicknames and even some customers. Readers could learn about Elizabeth Hudson, aka "Bet Slick"; Jenny Adams, aka the "Sheet-Iron Blonde"; and Bell Hooper, aka the "Drum Major." Apparently, the post office, which was on the northeast corner of Courthouse Square, was the main assignation point.

The controversy began when a mob burned down an alleged brothel run by a Mrs. Jack Conner (unrelated to William Conner) on October 10. It was on the south side of town near where many of the alleged houses were. The *Republican-Ledger* started the series on October 19, and it ran at various intervals until November 26.

The *Independent* accused the *Republican-Ledger* of libeling the city and called the editor a "rickety, addle-brained little nincompoop."[147] The *Republican-Ledger* responded by printing letters of support from various citizens. One of the points of controversy was that the *Republican-Ledger* had claimed that there were twenty-six brothels in Noblesville. The *Independent* was skeptical of this and said that it had only heard of six.

Interestingly, some of the women tried to answer the accusations by writing letters to the paper or talking to the editor. The *Republican-Ledger* did dismissive reports of this. However, looking at it from today's point of view, some of the statements that got printed raise questions of whether the accusations were true. The women were often poor and had little means to defend themselves. Eventually, enough newspapers were sold, and the controversy died out.

Unique Trials

A Ghost War

There was a time in Noblesville in late 1890 when "ghosts" appeared and frightened several families. The results were probably not what people had expected.

Events are a little hard to follow. Newspaper articles are the only source, and there were several articles with varying descriptions. There were also variations in the name of one of the central persons involved, whom the *Ledger* called James E. Lawhorn and the *Democrat* called James F. Lauhon. There were families with both spellings in Noblesville.

The incidents happened in the last half of November and the beginning of December. They were in an area called "Hell's Half Acre"—a neighborhood in the southeast part of town that had been developed by George Richwine. The Lawhorn/Lauhon family lived on Division Street.

The hauntings were underway by November 29, when there was a trial of James Lawhorn for assault against William Owens. Owens had been confronted on the street by Perry Bishop and accused of doing the hauntings. Their argument turned violent. When Bishop made a threatening gesture with a shovel, Owens pulled a knife. At that time, Lawhorn entered the fight by throwing rocks and brandishing a pistol. Lawhorn was arrested later and arraigned in court. The crowd at the trial was so large that the judge had to move the proceedings to the circuit courtroom.

Shots were heard in the neighborhood later that night. When Noblesville town marshal Frank Barnett investigated, he found Mrs. Lawhorn and a

Mrs. Phoebus. They said that they had seen figures draped in black and fired pistols to run them off. The next Monday night, the family of Robert Clayton was visited by ghosts, and Mrs. Clayton was terribly frightened. The Lawhorns were contemplating moving out of town.

The incidents came to a head on Thursday, December 4. First, a figure appeared at the window of Alice Adams. Then, as the Lawhorns were returning from the Craig grocery near the depot on Eighth Street, they overheard two men talking about ghosts. As Mrs. Lawhorn entered her yard at home, she saw two figures in white at the fence. She screamed, "There is that awful thing!" and ran toward the house. However, she jabbed her sternum against a pump handle that was horizontal and fainted from the pain. Mr. Lawhorn chased down the figures, which turned out to be two women—Mrs. Owens and Mrs. Harrison, wife of James Harrison. When Lawhorn confronted them, they told him, "We'll dress as we please." A doctor was called for Mrs. Lawhorn, and the women were arrested. They were arraigned in Judge Henry M. Caylor's court on charges of assault.

At the trial, Mrs. Harrison confessed her part in the full story:

> *Yes, sir, I was one of the ghosts. On that eventful night, I, in company with Mrs. Owens, threw sheets around ourselves and started out for a night of it. Our object was to frighten my husband and my brother-in-law, Price. Also sometime during the last few weeks I understood that Mrs. Lauhon had made boasts that no ghost could scare her, and perhaps that played an important part in the affair but I decline to make a positive statement to that effect. We fixed ourselves up so that I thought we looked pretty well considering everything. That's the whole story in a nutshell.*

The controversy over the trial caused a change of venue to Judge Willis Venable. A jury was empaneled, but they split on the verdict, with six for conviction and six for acquittal. Evidently, some sort of compromise or deal was reached by the plaintiffs and defendants because by Wednesday, December 10, all affidavits had been withdrawn.

In the end, the whole incident could be considered a prank that got out of control. After the case was dropped, the *Ledger* said, "This is perhaps not the best solution of the difficulty. While the parties were probably not able to pay a heavy fine without seriously embarrassing themselves, there perhaps should have been something done to have deterred any one from repeating the fun."[148]

Putting a "Lid" on Candy: The "Blue Laws," Part I

At the turn of the century, Noblesville had a statewide reputation for strict enforcement of Sunday closing laws, otherwise known as Blue Laws. These were laws passed by the state legislature about regulating activities on a Sunday, such as closing businesses. Noblesville's reputation was highlighted by two well-publicized cases that almost took this to the point of absurdity.

In 1907, the City of Noblesville banned selling candy and sodas on Sundays. Newspapers called it the "Candy Ban" or "Soda War." Mayor E.C. Wilson said, "This reform movement is not a sudden fancy. I have three years to serve and I intend to see to it that the Sunday laws are observed." He put a halt to sales in a July 26 order that covered ice cream, soda water, candies and chewing gum. He also closed the meat markets and said that housewives could just store meat purchased on Saturday in the icebox overnight. The newspapers said that he put a "lid" on things, and this became a buzzword in later articles.[149]

While some merchants objected, others obeyed. Customers went to other towns like Cicero for ice cream. In addition to the above, the mayor had closed cigar stores three weeks earlier. However, cigar vending machines had been recently installed on the interurban cars, and these got much use. In Noblesville, candy stores and soda shops were hit the worst. A photograph of children in front of one of the closed stores was staged for the Richmond newspaper.[150]

One of the largest and most popular of the confectioners was Dold's Candy, which first opened as the Candy Kitchen at 34 South Ninth Street in 1897. Other merchants backed John Dold to open and defy the ban. He did on August 11, and he and his wife, Marie, were arrested by Noblesville Police Department patrolman Frank Barnett. Barnett had left the city marshal's office in 1900 and was appointed as a police officer in March 1907.[151]

Advertisement for Dold's candy store. Hamilton County Times, *July 21, 1904.*

This was to be a test case, so the Dolds were released without bond, and their trial was held quickly. County Prosecutor Cassius Gentry brought the case, which was to be tried in the mayor's court.[152] Because of the obvious conflict of interest, the mayor was recused, and local attorney W.S. Christian was appointed judge. He and a jury of twelve men heard the case. Patrolman Barnett and John Dold were the only people to testify. The jury was unable to reach a decision, and the case was eventually dropped.[153]

The Sunday Baseball Trial: The "Blue Laws," Part II

The 1908 Noblesville baseball team had an eighteen-year-old first baseman, Clarence Wyant. Son of a local house painter and a top athlete in high school, in July 1908 he would be up against an opponent tougher than any big-city pitcher—the state Blue Laws.[154]

In April 1908, a Civic League was formed in Noblesville. Its goal was the continued moral improvement of the city. Its members stated that they would accomplish this by pushing for the enforcement of laws that had been only selectively enforced in the past. The first law that they chose was one that had been created fairly recently.[155]

The State of Indiana had passed a law against Sunday baseball in March 1905. It was part of a general law on Sabbath-breaking and was grouped in with laws on pornography and prostitution. It was challenged at every session of the legislature after that. The first test of the baseball law had been a trial held in Greenfield, Indiana, in October 1905. That player had been found guilty, and the case went to the appellate court, where it was upheld.[156]

One way that the baseball teams attempted to get around the Blue Laws was to hold their games in venues that could be used for other events as well. Then the public would not be "charged admission" to the game. The fee they paid was simply to enter the stadium, and the fact that a baseball game happened to be in progress was merely a coincidence. In Noblesville, the team used the county fairgrounds on the west side of town. The local paper asked sarcastically if people were paying twenty-five cents to view the "remains of the once famous frog ponds of that classic park." Since people were paying money to see the baseball team play at the county fairgrounds, and since the team would often play on a Sunday, this seemed like a clear violation. The Civic League filed an affidavit with the county prosecutor's office to have the case tried in the county circuit court. The trial was set for the last week of July.[157]

Noblesville 1908 baseball team. Clarence Wyant is seated at far left. *Hamilton County Historical Society.*

The county prosecutor, Cassius Gentry (who would later go on to have a long career as a judge), was reluctant to try the case. He didn't press charges until the political pressure became too strong. The trial was presided over by Justice of the Peace Joel Stafford and had a full twelve-man jury. Clarence Wyant may have been chosen as the defendant because of his experience doing mock trials in high school. He was represented by George Shirts, a grandson of some of the first settlers of the county. There were three witnesses called: George Stevenson; one of the fans who had seen the game; and Clarence himself. After the testimony was taken, the prosecution and defense attorneys gave their final arguments. Interestingly, George Shirts's closing argument barely mentioned guilt or innocence. He talked instead about the public embarrassment that the Civic League was causing the town. The jury was then recessed and, after fifteen minutes of deliberation, returned a finding of not guilty.[158]

The local paper referred to the Noblesville trial as a "test case" and a "friendly suit," but there were still hard feelings about it. After the trial, a local minister gave a strong sermon about moral failures in the town. However, he was fighting a losing battle. Interestingly, Mayor Wilson officially lifted the candy ban in July 1908. He claimed this was on the advice of doctors, who said that sodas and ice cream were beneficial to one's health during the summer.[159]

The Sunday baseball law was revoked by the state legislature in 1909.[160] Society was changing its views about professional sport. In 1908, Indiana native Albert Von Tilzer wrote the music to the song "Take Me Out to the Ball Game." Then in 1910, William Howard Taft began the tradition of the president throwing out the first pitch of the baseball season. The game was now the national pastime and had become a respectable way to spend an afternoon. And today, although it still has the occasional scandal, at least no one worries about the day on which it's played.

Part V

CIRCUSES, THEATERS AND MOVIES

Frank Stark

Circuses, Part I

It's understood that circuses invented many modern advertising practices. Posters, parades and publicity stunts were all part of attracting ticket buyers. The local area experienced a unique attempt in the nineteenth century that probably wouldn't be repeated today but did show some creativity.

Hamilton County has had its share of circus performers. Many of them were people who worked in the background areas of the circus, such as Bandmaster Robert Jamison (1864–1908) and valet/cook Henry Whitman (1885–1960). Some worked on the edges of the main show, such as medicine show performer Rufus Kellam (1883–1963).

However, the one performer who stands out for his inadvertent contribution to promotion was Frank Stark (1842–1862), a Noblesville man. He was a circus acrobat who fatally injured himself in an attempt to perform a daring feat. According to the *Daily State Sentinel* of August 11, 1862, Stark was in Indianapolis and had told a group of friends that he had performed a triple somersault while with a circus in Canada. This is actually a very dangerous stunt and had only been first successfully done by anyone in practice in 1839. Several performers had broken their necks attempting it before an audience. It was not done successfully in performance until 1881. His friends tried to discourage him. However, Stark was insistent. A $100 bet may have had something to do with it.

A springboard was set up in a grassy lot northwest of the city. As the *Sentinel* said, "At the first leap he timed twice and a half, when his hands slipped and fell, his forehead striking the ground, but he saved himself from injury by throwing out his hands. At the second attempt he went over twice and fell upon the back part of his head and shoulders, severely injuring his spine." He lingered for a short while in pain and then died.[161]

The story picks up again in 1869, when the Adam Forepaugh circus, one of P.T. Barnum's great rivals, was touring the country and made a stop in Noblesville. The *Noblesville Register* reported that on the evening before their performance, the circus band went to Riverside and played a dirge over Stark's grave in Riverside Cemetery. When asked why they did this, they told the reporter that "since Stark was killed, the band of every show that has passed here has paid similar honor to his remains." The *Register* commented on how touching it was that they would honor a departed comrade in this manner, particularly since they had probably not known him personally. They also played over the grave of a local horse dealer named Hamblin Shepard (1822–1867) who had sold horses to the circus.[162]

This happened again in 1878 when the Sells Brothers' circus was in town. The circus band performed a dirge, put flowers on Stark's grave and shed a few tears. While these tributes were very touching, it didn't seem to occur to anyone at the paper or in town that this would be a way for the circus owners to get some free advertising. Tasteless as this may seem, this sort of thing was typical practice for a circus of the time. Forepaugh was considered to be as much a publicity genius as Barnum. However, whatever the owners' motives might have been, the performers were probably very sincere.[163]

Interestingly, one of the staff members of the Forepaugh circus who might have planned this was John J. Justice (1825–1880), who also was originally from Noblesville. He was an "agent" or "advance man," which was the person who came to an area before the circus to make arrangements and do promotion. He was the one responsible for getting advertisements in the paper and putting up posters all over town. Although Stark never worked for the Forepaugh circus, Justice may have actually known him and the story of his death.[164]

There was yet another local connection to the 1869 Forepaugh show: Warren N.E. Slate, aka Professor Harry Slate (1834–1881). He was a clown, tumbler and ringmaster with the circus. In later years, during the off-season, he did sleight-of-hand magic work in New York with his wife, one of the daughters of Judge Earl Stone of Noblesville. Slate had married her in 1870. He may have owned property in Noblesville and did some special charity performances here, but he died in New York and was buried there.[165]

As traveling circuses began to fade, there was less need for this kind of activity, and Stark was slowly forgotten. Still, the events around his death make for an interesting view of nineteenth-century attitudes about how to get the word out.

Antonio Migasi

Circuses, Part II

One of the most famous circus performers connected to Hamilton County was Antonio Guilielmo Migasi (1820–1902), an acrobat who was part of an internationally famous pioneering circus family. The Antonio Brothers Circus was formed in the early nineteenth century and was one of the first real circuses in the United States.

The patriarch of the family, also called Antonio, was born in Turin, Italy, in 1795. He became skilled in acrobatics, feats of strength and slack-rope performing. He premiered in England in 1816 and was known as "Il Diavolo Antonio." He married an English woman, Christiana Crockford, in February 1818, and they had five children: daughter Margaretta (b. May 31, 1818) and sons Antonio (who performed under the name of Guilliame), Lorenzo (b. 1823), Augustus (b. 1826) and Alphonso (b.1828). Il Diavolo Antonio first appeared in New York in 1833 and moved permanently to the United States not long after that.

His sons took up the occupation of acrobats and formed a troupe that became the Antonio Brothers Circus. They would partner with other troupes to create a complete show involving animal acts and clowning. At one point, Guillaime did an act called the "Fire King," which involved performing acrobatics while standing in the middle of a pyrotechnic display called the "volcano." They performed all over the United States in the 1850s, including states like Iowa and Minnesota, where they were the first circus ever to visit the area.[166]

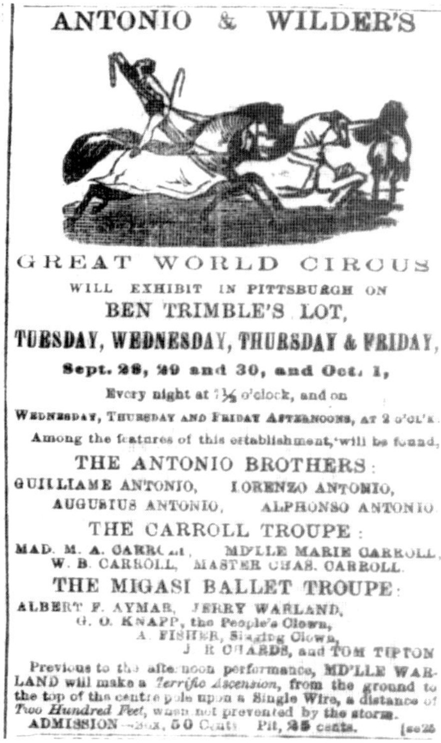

Above: Advertisement for Antonio Brothers Circus. Pittsburgh Daily Post, *September 27, 1858.*

Right: Advertisement for Antonio Brothers Circus. Weekly Pantagraph, *September 4, 1861.*

The brothers performed until 1862, when they sold the circus and took up regular careers in St. Louis. In 1871, Guilliame, now called Antonio, was running a livery stable in St. Louis and was quite successful. However, in September of that year, a horse he was driving became spooked, ran away with the carriage and crashed. Antonio was severely injured, and it was thought that there might be brain damage.[167]

He moved to Hamilton County so that he could be cared for by his wife's family. She was Catherine Sperry, and her family had lived in the county for some time. Antonio and Catherine had met when his circus was wintering at the Hamblin Shepard farm near Strawtown. Shepard was known for breeding horses and sold many of them to the circuses. Antonio had other local acquaintances as well. At one point, the advance man for the Antonio Brothers Circus was John T. Justice (mentioned previously). Antonio and Catherine's two daughters eventually married local men. Although his injuries were permanent, Migasi lived for another thirty years. He was quiet and kept to himself but was well liked in the community. He died in 1902 and is buried in Strawtown Cemetery.[168]

John H. Wise

Noblesville Playwright

John H. "Johnnie" Wise (1860–1941) was born on a farm near Carmel and came to Noblesville in 1873. He married in 1882 and had one child. In 1888, he started a newsstand and stayed in that business for the rest of his life. Apparently, he never had many financial problems. His mother-in-law inherited a large sum of money in 1891, which presumably came down through the family. He had a nice house on Clinton Street and a farm on North Cumberland Road. When he died, he left an estate of $13,000.

He was also in the theater business. He started the Home Theater on Logan Street in 1906, which was supposedly the first movie house in Noblesville (although the Wild Opera House had been showing short films with plays for several years). The theater later became the Vaudette and had live acts to go with the films. Wise eventually sold that theater and worked with other businessmen in 1919 to create the Olympic Theater, later renamed the Diana.[169]

A biographical article in 1928 pointed out that there were two sides to his character—the solid businessman and the idealistic writer. He started writing early in his life and had a short story published in a Chicago paper in 1881. His playwriting career began in 1897 when he wrote and copyrighted *Forsaken: An Emotional Play*. A production was mounted at the Wild Opera House on November 2, and the cast was:

Vivian Vane, the country girl who is forsaken—Leota Fodrea
Gerald Wayne, the false lover—Charles W. Craft
Edith Reid, the city girl and unloved wife—Marie Dold
Eva Vane, Vivian's sister—Maude K. Wise (the playwright's daughter)
Sam Patch, the farmhand—Hugh G. Brock
Gypsy Madge, an old fortuneteller—Daisy Fariss
Mrs. Vane, Vivian's mother—Florence E. Ross (the company manager's wife)
Mary, Edith's maid—Maude K. Wise (doubling)
A city thief—Hugh G. Brock (doubling)

The company manager was William Ross. Thirty years later, Leota Fodrea would be remembered as one of the most beautiful and talented girls in town, and it was said that she did a "wonderful portrayal" in the play. According to both of the newspapers in town, her acting and singing carried the show, despite the fact she had never been on stage before and had only graduated from high school in May.

The show was a huge success; it sold out almost immediately, and a second night was added. On the opening night, the playwright was called out for a speech at the end of the second act, and a large floral tribute was given to him. The cast had a photo taken, and the manager talked about taking the show on the road. This never materialized.[170]

The sequel to the play, *Forgiven*, was written and copyrighted in 1898. The two plays were then performed together at the opera house—*Forsaken* on Tuesday, November 15, and *Forgiven* on Wednesday, November 16. The cast members were many of the same people who had performed the year before. This time, the house was only about half full for each show, but the actors did a good job. Ernest Carey and Fred Johnson were pointed out. There was backstage drama as well. William Ross and Daisy Fariss abandoned their respective spouses and ran off together. The newspaper made the comment, "And so this will be a sequel to 'Forsaken' that will not be 'Forgiven.'" This led local ministers to preach about the "wickedness of theater." In the end, ticket receipts covered the production expenses but not payment to the actors.[171]

Portrait of John Wise used as the frontispiece for the published version of the play *Forsaken*, 1898.

In 1901, Wise combined the two plays, rewrote them and retitled the final product *Man's Work*. He had the Gentry Stock Company, a professional troupe performing at the opera house in April 1903, mount a production. (It's unknown if he paid them or just talked them into it.) Despite having only a few hours of rehearsal, the local paper said it was an enjoyable show.[172]

Wise revived the play in 1908 with a three-week tour around Indiana. He hired professional actors from Chicago and rehearsed them at the Vaudette. The show opened in Martinsville on September 5 and then went to Greencastle (September 11), Lafayette (September 14) and Noblesville (September 19). The Martinsville production got a short promotional piece in *Billboard* magazine. Despite a good reception back in Noblesville, the *Indianapolis Star* said that the audiences were small, and the tour became unprofitable.[173]

The plays are typical melodramas of the time and would be considered too over-the-top for modern audiences. The plot is too convoluted to go into detail here, but it's about a married man who falls in love with another woman but doesn't want to give up his wife. He abandons the other woman and (spoiler alert) she dies. He is eventually forgiven and marries her sister after his wife dies (!). Even though *Man's Work* was called "the great woman's play," the attitude toward women is not up to today's standards.

Berta Jones

Woman Playwright

Berta Jones was born Alberta Haworth on February 21, 1877, to Albert Haworth and his wife, Sarah (Bray). She married Alva Curtis "A.C." Jones on December 31, 1895, and by then, she was known as Berta. In the 1900 census, A.C. was running a dry goods store in Hortonville and the couple had a two-year-old son named Paul.

Berta had apparently had literary aspirations for some time, since a newspaper article said that she was "a writer of more than local reputation, many of her stories being published in Eastern magazines."[174] None of these stories has been found yet. Then, in 1901, at the age of twenty-four, something inspired her to take things to another level. She decided to write and produce a play.

The play was titled *Rashleigh*. It was the story of the son of an English aristocratic family who falls in love with a beautiful country woman with no title or money and marries her. His family is horrified by this and forces them to separate. The country woman is driven away, and the son is made to marry a woman with equal social stature. However, he cannot forget the first woman and (spoiler alert) finally returns to her just as she dies of a broken heart. The play has some interesting similarities to the play by John Wise that was discussed previously. Wise's daughter Maude was an actress in both shows.

The director was Maude Wagner of Noblesville, who also played the female lead. The male lead was Charles White of Indianapolis performing under the name of "Clarence Cooper." Other actors were Addie Liner, Alice

Wright, Ernest Carey, Harry Wagner and A.C. Jones. Berta also designed the scenery. She and her husband were so determined to put on this play that they skipped a trip to California that had been planned.[175]

While the rehearsals were held in the Wild Opera House in Noblesville, the premiere was performed at the Grand Opera House in Anderson on the evening of December 18. A special train was run on the Midland Railroad to take Westfield and Noblesville residents to see the show.[176] As it happened, Governor Winfield T. Durbin was from Anderson and was visiting his home at that time, so he attended with his wife and State Senator Thomas J. Lindley of Westfield. Afterward, Lindley sent a message to the *Noblesville Ledger* saying:

> *The drama "Rashleigh" has been given at the Opera House at Anderson, the curtain is down, and Mrs. Jones, the author, is receiving congratulations at all hands. The performance was indeed quite creditable. Miss Maude Wagner and Mr. Ernest Carey especially did themselves proud. Governor and Mrs. Durbin came from Indianapolis to witness the play and both expressed much pleasure at the entertainment.*[177]

Unfortunately, the critics did not agree with Lindley. The *Anderson Morning Herald* said, "It had some merits of a good theatrical production, but, like the majority of plays, has its weak points."[178] The *Indianapolis News* headline read, "Mrs. Jones' Play Is Not Particularly Strong" and went on to say, "The members of the cast were nervous and the performance lacked smoothness and finish, the company lacking anything out of the ordinary in talent."[179]

The play was repeated at the Wild Opera House on December 21. This time, the *Ledger* repeated the *News* review while adding, "There appears to be material in Mrs. Jones' story for a play of merit, but it is not well arranged."[180] The *Noblesville Democrat* said, "For an amateur production in the hands of home theatrical talent, the play was a most worthy and successful one. But for a professional effort, it displayed many rough edges."[181] Regrettably, there are no known copies of Berta's play existing today, so a judgment can't be made.

After this, we hear no more about Berta Jones and the theater. By 1907, the family had moved to Gary, where Berta died on January 10, 1918, of appendicitis. Her body was brought back to Hamilton County and buried in Hinkle Creek Cemetery.[182]

SHERIDAN'S LOST EPIC

"The Dairy Queen"

Product placement is now a standard method for getting funding for movies, but the Indiana Condensed Milk Company in Sheridan beat the trend by decades. In 1919, it put up the money for a feature-length film that would show how the company was in the vanguard of modern diary practices. The result was called *The Dairy Queen*.

The January 3, 1920 *Noblesville Ledger* described the movie as "a Hamilton County picture produced, written, directed, and played by Hamilton County people, with scenes about Noblesville, Sheridan, Carmel, and Tipton. Over ten thousand people shown. Three months in preparation. A cast of fifty characters. A fascinating love story. One hundred good laughs."

It was written and directed by two local men: Frank E. Davidson, the pastor of Sheridan Christian Church, and Nola E. Boyer, a teacher and school superintendent who was then working for the Indiana Condensed Milk Company. They were probably helped by Herbert Tapp, a local actor and playwright, who also played one of the lead roles in the movie and later would manage the Hippodrome Theater. The Milk Company paid for the $5,000 budget, and the film included an appearance by the company president, W.T. Wilson.

The plot was explained in the November 4, 1919 *Noblesville Ledger*:

> *The story is that of a young farmer boy, disgusted with the old way in which things have been running on his father's place, attends the dairy picnic accompanied by his sweetheart, Miss Mary Jones, which character*

Left: Magazine cover showing Irene Willwerth in character for the film *The Dairy Queen*. The Jersey Bulletin and Dairy World, *December 3, 1919*.

Below: Advertisement for the film *The Dairy Queen*. Noblesville Ledger, *October 31, 1919*.

> *is taken by Miss Irene Willwerth. John is inspired to venture on the sea of experience in the dairy business. He does not sail alone. The sailing was not always smooth for there were threatening storms, but Mary made a fortunate investment in a good dairy cow and they came out ahead of the game and were happy.*

The first scenes were filmed in August at the Milk Company annual "dairy picnic," which was a huge event. There was much media coverage of the female lead, whose father was a prominent merchant in town. In December, she was featured on the cover of a leading magazine for dairy farmers. Curiously, there wasn't much coverage of the male lead, Joseph McGee "Joe" Parr. He was a Sheridan High School graduate and a salesclerk who boarded at the Willwerth family home. He eventually moved to California.[183]

The featured cast was:

Irene Willwerth (age nineteen)—Mary Jones
Joshua G. Antrim (age fifty-three)—Joseph Jones
Cora Antrim (age forty-three)—Mrs. Jones
Joe Parr (age twenty)—John Hawkins
Herbert Tapp (age forty-one)—Hiram Hawkins
Madge Johnson (age thirty)—Mrs. Hawkins
Marion Ross (age nineteen)—Little June Hawkins

The final length of the film was four reels (which was probably about forty minutes). This would be considered feature length in 1919. It premiered at the Sheridan Christian Church on October 21 and ran for two nights. There was a bigger premiere at the Wild Opera House in Noblesville on November 3. The film had a special score written by Oscar Kaufman, a prominent midwestern violinist.[184]

It was recut and rereleased in December 1920. Filming began for a follow-up movie about raising Jersey cows, but it was never made. While this film was a serious effort, there is no evidence that *The Dairy Queen* was ever picked up by a national distributor and shown elsewhere. The print of the film is probably long gone—most likely the nitrate disintegrated decades ago. It would be an interesting film to see today.[185]

Otis F. Bart

A Wild West Performer

An interesting connection between Noblesville and Hollywood is due to a local man, Otis F. Bart, who knew the famous silent movie cowboy star Tom Mix. This was highlighted in an article that appeared in the *Noblesville Ledger* on May 28, 1925, titled "A Noblesville Man Meets Two-Gun Movie Hero—Ote Bart and Tom Mix Chat over Old Days on Pacific Coast." It describes how Bart put away his supplies for his occupation of billposting (pasting up advertising posters on buildings) and went to Indianapolis to see Mix, who was in town on a promotional tour. When Bart arrived in the city and got close enough to talk to Mix, at first Mix didn't recognize him. Then Bart said, "Have you heard what Jim Gable is doing?" at which point Mix remembered him. The article says that the three men had all been part of a Wild West show in Seattle, Washington, in 1910. Mix then sat down with Bart, and they chatted for a while. A reporter asked Bart about it later that week, and he said, "I remember very distinctly when I staked Mix for $15 to carry him through payday the next week. I thought about asking him for a return of the favor when I saw him on Wednesday. I suspect that he had the money to make the loan in the event that I had asked him for it."

The joke in this statement is that in 1925, Tom Mix was one of the highest-paid movie stars in Hollywood and was making as much as $7,500 a week. It's actually rather astonishing that Bart was even able to speak with Mix. According to the *Indianapolis News* article of May 27 that covered Mix's visit, there were thousands of people in attendance, as well as Indiana governor Ed Jackson and Mayor Lew Shank of Indianapolis.

So how did a Noblesville billposter come to work with a top movie star? Otis Bart had led a rather interesting life. He was born on a farm in Boone County on December 25, 1887. At some time, he left Indiana and by 1908 was in Nebraska as a private in Company H of the Second Regiment of the Nebraska National Guard, where he served for three years. He was known for his shooting skills and attained the level of marksman.

The Wild West show that the two men worked in had actually been organized in 1909 by Tom Mix himself. (There are a few errors in the *Ledger* article—whether on the part of the reporter or of Otis Bart isn't known.) The show was done in conjunction with the Alaska-Yukon-Pacific Exposition. "Jim Gable" was probably actually William J. Gabriel (aka "Cheyenne Bill"), a well-known Wild West show promoter who had worked with Buffalo Bill and helped Mix put the show together. Since Mix was running the show, it's pretty unlikely that Bart would have had to loan him money before payday.

The *Ledger* article states that Bart was with the Wild West company as an expert shot. This is very likely, not only because of his military service but also because of the fact that he was well known as a sharpshooter when he returned to Indiana. Bart may be one of the men in a 1909 photograph of some of the performers in the show.

Bart eventually returned to Indiana, married Golda Altum in 1912 and settled in Noblesville. However, somewhere in his travels, he lost an eye. This seemed to have no effect on his shooting ability. He was called up for the draft in World War I but was rejected because of his eye. Still, in 1920, he was part of a twenty-man picked rifle team that represented Indiana at a national target match at Camp Perry, Ohio.[186] There is a photograph that may show him giving a demonstration in Noblesville at the old Horse Show grounds at the corner of Monument and Tenth Streets.

Bart died in 1930, just five days after his birthday, due to complications from surgery. In his obituary, it said he was regarded as the best rifle shot in the county and that one of his hobbies was to travel to northern Michigan and Canada in the fall to hunt big game. It also said that one of his other hobbies was working with local organizations on charitable giving projects.[187] This was something that he shared with Tom Mix. On his 1925 visit, one of the first places that Mix went was Riley Children's Hospital.

The Community Players

Noblesville's African American Theater Troupe

A new piece has been added to the history of theater in Noblesville, thanks to research done by Lezli R. Davis. Twentieth-century theater groups in the city started with the Noblesville "Little Theatre" society, which did shows between 1929 and 1935. Along with this, Noblesville High School produced plays and had a Thespian Society. In 1951, an amateur troupe did a production of *The Man Who Came to Dinner* that was well received. Then in June 1965, the Hamilton County Theater Guild was organized. The new information is that, in the midst of this, the African American residents of Noblesville created a theater troupe that tackled difficult plays and performed with a diverse cast. The group was called the Community Players.

The key motivator of the organization seems to have been a man named Jack D. Brinson, who was not a native of Hamilton County. The newspaper said that he had attended Northwestern University and had directed productions at Karamu House, a nationally recognized African American theater organization in Cleveland, Ohio. He may have been the same person who was a theater student at Sacramento University in 1946. It's not known why he was in Noblesville.[188]

The Community Players chose serious and complex plays to perform. This may have been in response to the portrayal of African Americans in the minstrel shows put on by the local white community as charity fundraisers. Despite good intentions, these shows were offensive to African Americans and to modern sensibilities.

The first show produced was *Present Laughter*, a sophisticated comedy written by Noel Coward. It was staged on June 28, 1956, at the Noblesville Junior High School gym. Wilma Battey Avery played the female lead, with many of the other cast members coming from Indianapolis. We don't have a copy of the actual cast list, but newspaper accounts give the following names:[189]

Wilma Battey Avery—Liz Essendine
William H. Strong Jr.—Garry Essendine
Delores L. Porter—Monica Reed
Jack Brinson—Roland Maule
Kenneth White—Fred, the valet
Gloria Ramona Reeves—Daphne Stillington?
Jeanne E. Hull—Joanna Lyppiatt?
Omar K. Nelson
Jacque N. Sneed
Barbara Sneed

Ticket sales were conducted by Jacqueline Williams, Maizie Glover, Murphy White and Kenneth White. The furniture for the set was loaned by the Noblesville Furniture Company, which was owned and operated by Vin Haggan. The *Ledger* newspaper gave a very complimentary review of the performance that said that "theater-goers were given a treat" and that the show was "highly acclaimed," with the audience "eagerly looking forward" to the next production.[190]

Ernest Butler. *1952 Noblesville High School yearbook.*

Eunice White. *1944 Noblesville High School yearbook.*

The second production was *Summer and Smoke*, written by Tennessee Williams. It was staged on August 31, 1956, at the Logan Theater, and newspaper accounts give the cast and crew as follows:[191]

Eunice White—Alma Winemille
Ernest Butler Jr.—John Buchanan Jr.
Wilma Battey Avery
Natalie Glover
Kenneth White
Betty Scott
Norman Grundy
Hazel Barber
Harry Taylor
Duane Odle
Jim Tener
Steve Thom
Thelma Dean Vandiver

Nancy Taylor—Production Manager
COSTUMES:
Maizie Glover
Connie Holman
Harriet Howard
Alice Jane Asher
Judi Howard
Betty Parrott
Barbara Parrott
Phyllis Scott
Marguerite Bush
TECHNICAL CREW:
Robert White
George Barker
Jerry Avery

An interesting point was the diversity of the cast. The first play had Omar K. Nelson, who was white. The second play had a group of white high school students in the cast and crew—Harry Taylor, Duane Odle, Jim Tener, Steve Thom, Thelma Dean Vandiver, Nancy Taylor and George Barker. It's not known how the students became involved in the production. There is irony in the use of the Logan Theater for the show. The theater had started as the U.S. Theater in the 1920s as a pro–Ku Klux Klan business and ran Klan-related movies.[192]

The local newspaper again gave the show a good review. There had been a smaller audience than expected, but the paper said: "This young dramatic group is merely learning, as scores of similar entrepreneurs have learned again and again in Indiana, that the desire for culture is hard to come by and that it requires the combined and continued efforts of a community to create it."[193]

After the second production, the Players announced their planned season: *The Solid Gold Cadillac*, written by Abe Burrows; *Dial "M" for Murder* by Frederick Knott; *Kind Sir* by Norman Krasna (the play was later made into the Cary Grant–Ingrid Bergman movie *Indiscreet*); *Street Scene* by Elmer Rice; and *The Shrike* by Joseph Kramm. However, none was ever staged. Apparently, the group dissolved, and Brinson moved back to California.

Part VI

HOAXES AND MYSTERIES

The White River Sea Serpent

Fake news or newspaper hoaxes were regarded by some newspaper publishers as an income producer. One such appeared on page two of the *Noblesville Democrat* for July 15, 1892. Quoted in full, it says:

> *A Big Snake Story*
> *Last Friday morning Samuel Applegate and George Farris, two young men of this city whose reputation for truth and veracity cannot be questioned, saw a strange sight which they converse very freely about. They were driving north on the Cicero Pike between the Lake Erie car bridge and the wagon bridge when their attention was attracted towards White River when they noticed what they at first supposed to be a large dog splashing in the water. Closer observation changed their opinion as to the character of the animal. A few moments later they saw the entire body of the monster, which had the form of a huge serpent twelve feet in length and perhaps three feet in circumference with a forked tail. On catching a glimpse of a man, the animal immediately disappeared and has not been seen since. It is supposed that it came down White River from some larger body of water during the recent floods.*

The *Indianapolis News* had mentioned it in the July 12 paper with a short sentence: "Noblesville imagines a sea serpent is infesting the waters of White River."

The story was picked up by the *Greencastle Democrat* (July 23) and *Jasper Weekly Courier* (July 29) and had the same short mention in both newspapers: "A new kind of varmint, said to be twelve feet long, was seen in the river near Noblesville."

There are several facts to be examined in this story. The two witnesses, Applegate and Farris, seem to be normal people. Applegate was a thirty-two-year-old Cicero drayman (wagon driver) who later moved to Montana and died in a carriage accident in 1910. Farris was a twenty-four-year-old Noblesville tailor who later got patents for developing new kinds of clothing display racks and died in California in 1940.

The "Cicero Pike" is now Highway 19. The "Lake Erie car bridge" is the Lake Erie and Western Railroad bridge, which now has the walking bridge to get to Forest Park. The "wagon bridge" is the Logan Street bridge, which was a covered bridge at that point in time. It's curious that the men are described as driving north, but the story mentions the railroad bridge before the Logan Street bridge.

It is true that there were large floods in central Indiana in June 1892. This was the period when the neighborhood of Johnstown acquired its nickname. A new factory under construction in southwest Noblesville was destroyed by one of the rainstorms.

A newspaper in Vincennes reported a very similar story as happening near there in April 1892. There were also serpents reported in Clarksville in southern Indiana and Knightstown. Editors back then were not averse to stealing ideas that might sell more newspapers.

There was an expedition (of sorts) that tracked down the monster. The efforts were reported in the *Noblesville Republican-Ledger*, with the first article being on July 15, 1892:

> *Os Phelps, Will Fryberger, Al Decker, Will Freehafer, and Ed Royer drove across the country to Anderson Tuesday, carrying boats and fishing tackle in great abundance. They will launch their boat at Anderson and let it float while they fish on the way homeward. The fish stories they tell on their return will equal the snake story which appeared in Monday's* Democrat, *which was without a doubt a hallucination of a diseased mind brought on by an attack of Tizerism of the brain, and woe be unto his monstership if he falls in the way of the invincible quintet on their homeward float, because they are equipped to capture large game and it would be a fortune to them should they capture this monster alive and exhibit it under canvas.*

(No source can be found for the word "Tizerism." It might mean something political, as the two newspapers—the *Republican-Ledger* and the *Democrat*—were constantly at war, particularly about politics.)

As it turned out, the expedition was a success, with an article on July 22 headlined "The Monster Captured." The sub-headline read, "The Democrat's Sea Serpent Secured by the Big 5 Fishermen."

> *On Wednesday evening when Os Phelps, Will Fryberger, Al Decker, Allen Freehafer and Ed Royer were nearing their home landing from their two days' fishing excursion, just between the railroad and wagon bridges a sight met their eyes that chilled the blood in their veins—even the stout-hearted commander of the crew, Phelps, held his breath in dread of the monster. Its appearance was truly terrible. What seemed to be a living monster was plainly visible. It was twelve feet long, on its head were formidable horns, in its center it was several feet wide and the extremity of its tail was adorned by a bush, and as it rose and fell with the waves, the stoutest of the crew held their breath at sight of the terrific monster. After a few moments delay and hurried consultation they determined to capture it, having remembered the ghost story of their boyhood and the language, "No harm I'm sure can happen to the good," they separated, one of the boats approaching from the south, the other from the north. They approached it warily with bated breath, each eye strained to discover a vulnerable point, each brave heart trembling as to the result. Nearer and still nearer they approached until of a sudden, Freehafer made a bold dash forward and seized a horn of the monster. A shout of exultation and relief went up from each throat when they discovered the monster to be nothing but the skin of a defunct bovine that had caught on some trash which held it there. An unfortunate ending of what the local editor on the* Democrat *had pictured as an estray deep water monster that had found its way here during the late freshets.*

There is quite a bit of sarcasm and hyperbole in that story. What's more, the *Republican-Ledger* was so eager to score points that it overlooked the fact that the object found by the fishermen does not fit the description in the other paper. The *Democrat* said the monster had a forked tail and said nothing about horns. So, who knows? The White River Serpent might still be out there.

Airships—Real and Otherwise

Fantastic fiction, like that written by Jules Verne, has always been popular with the residents of Hamilton County. In 1882, the *Noblesville Ledger* ran the novel *Around the World in 80 Days* as a serial. A key feature in many of the stories is the idea of airships, giant gas-filled balloons or dirigibles that could travel for miles. In the 1890s, airships were considered a real possibility and a topic of much local discussion.

It began with extensive coverage of the 1891 E.J. Pennington airship in Chicago (which turned out to be a fraud). The airship was so popular that when the Wallace circus visited Noblesville in October 1892, it had a thirty-foot replica of the craft (probably non-flying). Interest in the replica ended locally when Pennington himself conducted an electric railway fraud in Noblesville in 1893.[194]

Another part of the Wallace show involved actual flight. Lorella Monntrose and her horse Montgolfier did a balloon ascension. Balloon ascensions were a common sight at fairs and festivals, where aeronauts—usually young women—would ascend to a height of one thousand feet and then parachute to earth. This was very dangerous, and there are many reports of fatal falls. Unlike today's hot air or helium-filled balloons, the balloons for the ascensions were hydrogen filled, a practice that continued until the *Hindenburg* disaster in 1937.[195]

The fascination with airships reached a peak in 1897 and led to one notable hoax. The *Ledger* did a front-page story on May 25, 1897, about a flying machine cruising over Courthouse Square and included an illustration. The

Left: Advertisement for Wallace circus showing the Essington airship. Hamilton County Ledger, *October 7, 1892.*

Below: A drawing that appeared in the local newspaper to promote an airship hoax. Hamilton County Ledger, *May 25, 1897.*

tone of the report and the reactions from prominent citizens were all done tongue-in-cheek and should have tipped people off to the joke. However, the newspaper had to confess to the hoax after people kept reporting signs of the ship.[196]

In August 1909, the *Noblesville Enterprise* reported on a huge glowing object hanging in the sky over the west side of Noblesville. As it seemed to be over the area known as Johnstown (which was the neighborhood that had most of the city's brothels), there were comments about Sodom and Gomorrah and divine retribution. However, an Indianapolis astronomer soon asserted that it was the planet Mars, which happened to be in close conjunction with Earth.[197]

The Riverside Cemetery Stone

One local oddity is the limestone marker on the south side of Riverside Cemetery marked "1824." It has no other markings and is not a gravestone. So, what is the story of the stone?

The first clue comes from an article in the *Noblesville Ledger* for May 24, 1942. It's titled "Stone Marks First Burial in Riverside" and talks about how the stone was moved to that spot in the autumn of the previous year and that the date had been engraved a few days prior. One of the cemetery trustees explained that the date was chosen to commemorate the first burial. If this is correct, we have no idea who the burial might be since the first marked grave is from 1830. So, it would appear that the stone is a twentieth-century object—except it seems very worn and battered for something created in the 1940s. Could it have come from someplace else? The answer is yes.

An article published the next day went into further detail about the cemetery history and mentioned that the stone was taken from the home of the late Newman D. Levinson on South Eighth Street. The Levinson family is a story unto itself (as has been covered before). However, in this case, the stone was available because the eldest son of the family, S.O. Levinson (the one who had been nominated for the Nobel Peace Prize), had given the site of the home to the city. His offer of the land to the city was typical of his charity work. The house was on the west side of the street between Conner and Maple just south of the alley. It was later the site of the city hall and is now a parking garage.

Limestone block in Riverside Cemetery with "1824" carved on the side. *Kurt Meyer photo.*

The next question is whether the stone was part of the Levinson house and was brought over after demolition. Probably not. Another *Ledger* article dated December 15, 1915, is titled "Recalls Old Landmarks in Noblesville." It describes how Polk Street (Eighth) was the main thoroughfare in town in the earliest days and most of the city's founding fathers had built homes along the road. In the 1840s, Judge William Garver had originally built the house that was later owned by the Levinsons. When he decided to fence in the front yard, he brought in some large stones and placed a low iron fence along the top. It was probably one of these loose stones that would have been available to haul to the cemetery a century later.

Where would Garver have gotten large stones like this? It turns out they were very handy. The 1915 article describes how he used stone left over from the attempted construction of the Central Canal. Funded by the 1836 Mammoth Internal Improvement Act, the canal was to connect Peru to Evansville, passing through Indianapolis. Very little was actually built before the project collapsed in the Panic of 1837 and the bankruptcy of the state of Indiana. The article said that the stones had been brought in to build a bridge; however, they may have been for an aqueduct like the one at the Whitewater Canal State Park. They had simply been abandoned when the project failed.

So, we have the early history of the town of Noblesville, canal engineering, state financial failure, and cemetery decoration and the Nobel Peace Prize all wrapped up in one object. That's a pretty epic story for a simple block of stone.

A Pioneer Murder Mystery

The killing of Benjamin Fisher is considered the first known murder in the county. The murder happened in Strawtown, which was a lively place at that time. It was the intersection of the Lafayette Trace and the trail that followed the White River from southern Indiana. The area was a convenient stopping point for travelers along the trails. A distillery and horse racing track were among the first businesses. At this point, Hamilton County had not been established, and the area was still part of the Delaware New Purchase.

There are no contemporary accounts of the murder; the earliest version available is from 1874, some fifty-three years after the incident. Fisher himself was born in 1791 in Pennsylvania and moved to Indiana after serving in the War of 1812. He was an early settler of the Fishersburg area, which would be named for him, in Madison County.[198]

The cause of the incident was a man named Philip Shintaffer (1776–1840), who ran a tavern in Strawtown (mostly known as a gin mill) and made his money by selling liquor to Native Americans. Later writers described him as a "notorious character."[199]

The standard version of the story begins in March 1821 when Shintaffer got into an argument with one of the local Native Americans, supposedly about watering down the liquor. Shintaffer knocked the Native American down and threw him into the fireplace, where he was severely burned and possibly died. The repercussions of the incident were felt in April, when Fisher and other farmers traveled to Strawtown to get axes sharpened at

Shintaffer's (who had the only grindstone in the area). A group of American Indians, possibly Miami or Pottawatomie, came to revenge themselves on Shintaffer for his actions the month before. Armed with knives and tomahawks, they attacked the tavern. The farmers responded with axes and whatever was at hand. They held off the Native Americans until Shintaffer was wounded and Fisher brained by a tomahawk. One Native American was killed, at which point the group fled.[200]

This narrative has been repeated for many years. Versions exist from possibly Shintaffer himself (second- or third-hand), Benjamin's daughter Mary Fisher Simmerman (1816–1884) and Benjamin's son Charles Fisher (1819–1912). One might assume these are reliable sources, despite Fisher's children being quite young when the incident occurred. However, oddities and discrepancies emerge when the story is analyzed by a historian. They include:

1. Different versions vary regarding the number of parties involved, but it generally comes out as four to six farmers holding off eight to twelve American Indian warriors. When one farmer was down and another wounded, the Indians abandoned the attack without completing what they came to do. This is pretty impressive hand-to-hand fighting skills on the part of the farmers and seems somewhat unlikely.
2. No guns were used; the Indians allegedly wanted silence, but nothing prevented one of the farmers from stepping into the trading post and picking up a firearm.
3. For unknown reasons, Fisher was buried in Strawtown, where he died—not sent home to his family and his own property, which was only about eight miles away. There was no official burial ground at that time in Strawtown and no reason why that site would have been preferred. The grave was apparently left unmarked. Later historians would mention a "low mound" with no headstone near what would become the Strawtown Cemetery. It could possibly be located with modern archaeological techniques.
4. The night after the killing, Shintaffer packed all of his goods and his family into a canoe and left the area. He followed White River to Greene County and settled there for a few years. The histories there refer to him as a man of "considerable notoriety" having a "quick temper" and often being the defendant in court cases. He left there in 1832 and finally settled in Cass County, Michigan.
5. Finally, despite this being a sizable attack on an isolated settlement, no record of an official reaction has been found. There was apparently no attempt to capture the perpetrators, even though during the War of 1812,

> soldiers would chase Native American warriors from Franklin County all the way to the area of modern Hamilton County. In 1824, three years after the Strawtown fight, Governor Ray would call out the militia because of the fears of retaliation for the Massacre on Fall Creek. But in this case—a wholesale assault and battle involving possibly twenty people and two deaths—nothing was said or done that appeared in any official documents.

Some of the people who remained to tell the story were interesting characters. Shintaffer himself was probably the source of the account written in 1874. One of the alleged participants was Jacob Hire, although he's not named in the earliest versions. He has a shadowy background and was sometimes partner with Shintaffer in business. He was the person who built the distillery and horse racing track. Later, he became overseer of the poor for White River Township (he had apparently built up a good client base). Another alleged participant was Jacob Colip, but he is also not mentioned in the earliest versions and there is no record of his being in Hamilton County until 1823. No other participants are named.

Charles Fisher, the son of Benjamin, was two years old at the time of the attack. While he was too young to have witnessed anything, he told this story often. He was known for his stories. For example, he said that he had the powder horn that his father carried in the War of 1812. He also said that he had the tomahawk that his father was killed with. And he said that he had pieces of his father's skull from the attack and would show these pieces to visitors.

In the final analysis, many of the stories don't appear to hold up, and it's not clear what actually happened. Native Americans have been accused of this crime for over two hundred years, even though they gained nothing from it—not even revenge. With the signing of the Treaty of St. Mary's in 1818, the American Indians were already leaving the state, so the motives in all cases seem a little unclear. No other possibilities seem to have been considered—including the short-tempered, violent man who fled the area immediately after the killing. No matter what else may have happened, Benjamin Fisher was in the wrong place at the wrong time and left a conundrum for future historians.

Going Viral in 1837

It's unpredictable what will catch the public's attention and make a person famous (or infamous) on the internet. Actually, that goes further back than you might think. During the election for Indiana state representatives in 1837, a Hamilton County writer used a turn of phrase that went international.

The newspapers of the time were looking at issues like the failure of the 1836 state transportation project, partially caused by a national financial crisis, which sent the state into bankruptcy. There were also concerns about the Seminole Wars in Florida, Texas independence and the death of King William IV of England, who was replaced by his niece Victoria.

Then on May 18, 1837, a letter appeared in the Noblesville newspaper named (appropriately enough) *The Newspaper*. It was from a person calling himself "Isaac Cachel" and announced his candidacy for the state legislature. He stated that his opponents were a "priest" and a lawyer and were therefore untrustworthy. He also said he would resolve the state financial issues by designating raccoon skins as the official currency.

He said that his qualifications for office were that "I believe that I was the first civilized man that skinned a coon, chased a deer, caught a bear or treed a wildcat on the west side of the White River." This statement is what got everyone's attention. Even at that time, it was an unusual résumé for a politician.

The name was occasionally spelled "Cachell," and there is no person by either of those names in any records from the period. While most people used pen names in the newspapers for anonymity, much like bloggers do today, this was probably meant to be a larger-than-life made-up character.

The phrase about his qualifications and his currency proposal caught the eye of someone at the *Indiana Herald*, which was a paper with a statewide readership, and it was reprinted there in June. The *Herald* report was picked up by the *Bloomington Post*, and it was off and running. The story appeared in Ohio, then New York, and by September, it had appeared in at least sixteen newspapers spread across the twenty-six states and various territories of the United States.

"Cachel" had been writing other letters to the local paper when he saw this response and decided to try to take it to the next level. He put a prospectus in the paper asking for money to write and publish a book of his adventures. The equivalent today would be something like GoFundMe. The prospectus ran for several weeks but was evidently unsuccessful.[201]

The story was still going viral, and in January 1838, it jumped the Atlantic Ocean, appearing in the *Caledonian Mercury* in Edinburgh, Scotland. A few days later, it was in the *London Times* and eventually was printed in ten different English, Welsh and Scottish papers. By this time, the original name had disappeared from the various transcriptions, so the British papers gave the character a new name of "Seth W. Dobble."[202]

The story achieved its furthest reach on February 26, 1838, when it appeared in the *Sydney Morning Herald* in Australia. It may have also appeared in European papers, but since the original name was dropped, language differences make it difficult to track. Back in Indiana, "Cachel" sent his last letter to the local paper in September 1838. Overall, besides the prospectus, there were just six actual letters, some of which are only known from transcriptions in other papers. The name never actually appeared on the ballot.

There was a renewal of interest in "Cachel" in the 1970s with the county sesquicentennial and the United States bicentennial. He provided the title for an excellent local history column by Georgianne Neal that ran in the *Noblesville Ledger* between 1978 and 1980. The first letter had said that "the coon catcher and the corn-planter" were the "real bone and sinner [sinew] of the country." Ms. Neal named her column "Coon Catchers and Corn Planters" and interviewed many elderly members of the community who have since passed away. By doing so, she created a resource that is still useful.

Modern internet databases have made it possible to find all of the letters and relevant articles. While it's unlikely the writer's true identity will ever be known, it's intriguing to think that one of the county's most famous pioneers was fictional.

THE MYSTERY OF JOSEPH MORSE

In one of the older parts of Crownland Cemetery, there is a gravestone that marks a mystery. It looks like a chess piece but is actually a variation on a sculpture of an urn. The years have knocked it slightly askew. It belongs to Joseph Jacobs Morse, a man who carried a secret for most of his life and took it with him to the grave. He was born in 1812 in Woodstock, Connecticut, to Charles and Sophia Morse. His father and Samuel F.B. Morse, the inventor of the telegraph and Morse code, were cousins. Joseph married Elizabeth Hill (1813–?) in 1833, but other than this, we can find very few primary sources with information about him.[203]

According to his obituary in the *Noblesville Ledger*, he left Connecticut in 1838. He spent several years in Kentucky along the Big Sandy River trading in furs, ginseng, honey and other things. He was a strong abolitionist and left Kentucky rather than deal with slavery. He came to Noblesville around 1866 and set up a watch repair business. He was said to be very friendly and outgoing and popular in the local community. He was known for his storytelling ability and strong opinions.[204]

He became very involved in a project in 1874 to create a park for the mineral spring that was on the riverbank south of where the judicial center is today. The pioneers had used the site for hunting; it made an excellent salt lick for deer. Morse claimed that the spring had restored his health after a bout of illness and sent samples to a laboratory to be analyzed. Ironically, the project stalled when his health took a turn for the worse. In 1876, he contracted erysipelas and was in poor health afterward. He died on May 30, 1877.[205]

Later aerial photograph of the site of the Lewellyn Spring, which Joseph Morse attempted to turn into a park. *1935 Noblesville High School yearbook.*

He had not communicated with his family in all the time since he had left Connecticut. In his obituary in the *Ledger*, it was mentioned that he rarely spoke about his past, and the writer commented, "It has been thought that he was the bearer of a painful secret." The reporter estimated the value of the estate at $5,000 to $6,000.

A September 17, 1940 *Ledger* article has some further details about Morse's last days. Before he died, he had asked his friend George Vestal to contact his family. A nephew came, settled the estate for the eastern heirs and put up the marker. However, an article found in a Chicago newspaper said that the estate was worth $10,000 and had been left to "J.W. Dunflinger" and "R.G. Lucas." There were two local men named John W. Durflinger, a carpenter, and Robert G. Lucas, a marble dealer. So perhaps the money was to continue construction of the mineral spring park. The spring was possibly covered over when the Conner Street bridge was built in the 1930s.[206]

There is no mention of Morse's wife in either of the 1877 articles. He hasn't been found in any of the census records between his birth and death. The man left almost no paper trail. So, what was his secret?

The Man Who Knew

While most people would be excited to be part of one mystery, there was a local man who was part of two. Richard Howard "Howe" Davidson (1829–1896) was a Noblesville businessman who ran a boot and shoe store, a hotel and some other local businesses. His good memory and eye for detail provided important clues for investigating crimes.

The first mystery happened in July 1885. A decomposed body was found in a field near Castleton by a farm worker. (There was some alarm, as a ghost had been seen near there in March.) After investigation, the body was determined to be a victim of a shooting affray. The person later charged with the murder claimed that he had been shot at by a stranger and then ran away after shooting back.[207]

The dead man's identity was a mystery until Davidson spoke up. He said that the man was John C. Moffit, an English immigrant who had worked for him. Davidson said that Moffit was "a very peculiar man" and described him in a July 18 article in the *Indianapolis News*:

> *He was evidently a gentleman who had seen better days. He had been in the British army up in Canada, up to 1857, when he deserted and went to England, staying there until 1865. Upon his return to this country, he traveled very extensively for a linen house in Scotland. From that time until within a few years he refused to give any account of his life, but it is probably the old story of privation and suffering, resulting from the use*

> *of whisky and opium, to which he was greatly addicted. After he came to Noblesville, he did all sorts of work, running errands, digging ditches and tending bar, and was employed by Mr. Davidson for some time at his hotel. Moffit, when his mind was unimpaired by drink, showed by his conversation and information that he was a learned man, educated in all the higher branches, and was a very entertaining talker.*

The next mystery was in April 1891, when some workmen were excavating a cellar for an addition to a house at the corner of Cherry and Fourteenth Streets. At about four to six feet deep, they came across a human skeleton in a sitting position with its back to the east. It was examined and found to be of an extraordinarily large man who was thought to be fairly young, as the teeth were relatively unworn. The *Democrat* newspaper did some further investigation and found some thought-provoking facts.[208]

They questioned "Bent" Smith, the workman who had found the skeleton, who showed them a small brass token with the characters "80," "W.W." and "5 cents" inscribed on it. At this point, Davidson stepped forward with an intriguing explanation. He had bought the land in January 1868, when it was mostly farm fields. He had noticed a fresh mound of dirt at that site at the time, but he had business matters to pursue and forgot about it. It was eventually plowed over and then built on.

Davidson then recalled that a year or so before he purchased the lot, a strange soldier was passing through town and stopped at the small farmhouse that was on the lot. The soldier was obviously fresh from the army and was carrying hundreds of dollars. It was Davidson's belief that this skeleton was the soldier. The brass token found with the remains supports this. It fits the description of something called a "sutler's token."

During the Civil War, merchants were issued licenses to travel with the regiments in order to sell them things not available from the army. These sutlers were often the only source of canned goods, writing paper and other luxuries for the soldiers. Since hard cash was rare at the battlefront, they would pass out tokens as change to be cashed in later. On this token, the "80" may have signified the regiment, "W.W." may have been the initials of the sutler and "5 cents" would probably have been the denomination.

Of course, how did the soldier end up in an Indiana cornfield? Since there was apparently no further work done on the remains, property ownership would be the next place to look. According to deed records at the Hamilton County Courthouse, a man named Abraham Nicholson (1806–1876) had owned the land from 1861 until December 1867. He had been settled in the county since 1839 and had been the founder of the town now known as Clarksville. However, during the 1860s, his life took some unusual twists.[209]

In April 1864, he and his wife, Sarah, separated, despite having been married for over twenty years and having at least six children. Sarah received half of his landholdings, as well as their home in Clarksville. Abraham got the land in Noblesville. He then married Harriet Allison in Marion County on November 1, 1866. Harriet was from Ohio but had married her first husband in Hamilton County in 1853 (it's not known what happened to him) and was twenty years younger than Abraham. She is listed as his wife on the deed to the Noblesville property. A curious trail, but it unfortunately leads to no conclusions.[210]

So, while Davidson provided some clues, the mystery remained unsolved. However, it gives us an interesting glimpse into the lives of our ancestors and, in doing so, gives a unique twist on the old phrase about "skeletons in the closet."

A Poetic Mystery

Hamilton County has had its share of authors and poets, most of whom were only known locally. However, there may have been a poet who might have a wider audience—if this person actually existed. His or her name was Benoni P. Todd.

That name has appeared because of a letter supposedly from the Noblesville Home Literature Club to the *New York Sun* that was sent on December 2, 1904. The letter from Noblesville complimented the *Sun* for its willingness to promote Hoosier authors.

> *As humble citizens of this state, professing no talent ourselves for fine writing, we have long felt that we owed it to your great newspaper, as well as to ourselves, to make long past due acknowledgment to* The Sun *because of the enlightened interest, above referred to, which it has manifested in these productions of these fellow citizens of ours, which have undoubtedly, on many occasions, startled the literary world.*

The letter was answered on December 12. The newspaper said that it was grateful for the compliments and that the city had excellent taste in literature, and it ended by saying, "Noblesville has a park of authors, a lake, a sea, an ocean of poetry. She needs no more."[211]

However, it is a very odd exchange. Although Hoosier literature had giants like Lew Wallace, James Whitcomb Riley and Booth Tarkington, the *Sun* preferred to talk about poets like James Byron Elmore ("The Bard of

Alamo") or George Washington Sayler. Judging poetry is a question of taste, but the examples of Elmore's work in the essays seem to be very poor.

In the December 12 article, after discussing Elmore and Sayler, the paper mentions Benoni P. Todd as Noblesville's "own gifted verse smith" and quotes a section of his (or her) poetry:

Paris and Florence, Venice, Rome,
What are they to my Hoosier Home?
Praise not to me the City of Light;
She ain't a Noblesville, not by a sight!
Paris can't equal her by a week;
My Noblesville, my heart's delight!
Nestling soft on Cicero Creek,
Noblesville-on-the-White!

There is a problem—the name of Benoni Todd does not appear anywhere else except for one poem titled "Isolation" that appeared in a journal called *The Churchman* on July 9, 1881. There is nothing in the census records, cemetery records, county directories or newspapers around the country. This is possibly a pen name, which would make it impossible to track.

An interesting point is that there is no mention in the local papers for December 1904 about the article in the *Sun*. There is also no mention of a Home Literature Club. This is possibly all a grand hoax or satire. The language in the articles about James Elmore is laid on so thick that it's hard to tell. It may be an early twentieth-century version of an article in the *Onion*. The whole thing may have been some sort of huge joke; Elmore and Sayler were mocked in their own day for their ham-handed poetry.

So, is Benoni P. Todd an undiscovered Hamilton County artist or the takeoff point for satire?

The Missing Bridegroom

Clickbait in 1911

Although we may think of viral stories as a recent phenomenon, the notion of an odd story picked up and spread around existed long before anyone wrote "and you'll never believe what happened next!" Hamilton County is no stranger to this. An intriguing example involves a man named Eugene Woodmansee from Urbana, Illinois, who came here in 1867. Somehow, he met and fell in love with Sarah Vert, the daughter of the Castleton postmaster. Eugene proposed marriage twice, and the second time, Sarah accepted. Her father bought them a farm on Little Chicago Road, and the wedding was set for August 15.

Woodmansee arrived in town on August 14 aboard the Peru and Indianapolis Railroad. It had been a long trip; the only route from Urbana went across Illinois and Indiana to Peru, where you had to change trains and go south. There were only four trains a day through Noblesville. Eugene stayed at local hotel that night and was supposedly carrying a large amount of cash. The wedding was set for eight o'clock in the evening. Around seven o'clock, the minister ran into Woodmansee on the Courthouse Square. They had a pleasant conversation in which the minister offered to loan the couple a buggy, and Woodmansee laughingly said that he had already hired one. Then, when the conversation ended, Woodmansee walked away, turned the corner of a building and disappeared.

The house at the farm was all set up for the wedding. Candles were lit, and guests were there. The time came and went—first eight o'clock, then nine and beyond—no groom. The bride started to become frantic

SCENE OF NOBLESVILLE MYSTERY

The cross in the door shows where the first bones were found under the old house at Noblesville. The cross in the yard indicates where the trunk was unearthed.

Above: Photograph of the site of the discovery of Eugene Woodmansee's body. Indianapolis News, *January 12, 1911.*

Right: Image of Eugene Woodmansee's mother. Indianapolis Star, *May 21, 1911.*

and was consoled by family and friends. Most guests eventually drifted off, assuming he had stood her up. However, after searches were begun, it became obvious that he was completely gone. His family in Illinois was contacted, and they hired a Chicago detective. There were no signs and no evidence of anything, so eventually they gave up. As time passed, the memory of the event started to fade. Eleven years later, Sarah Vert married another man, Daniel Jones, and died ten years after that. Her husband outlived her. When he died, he was buried in a different place—in Westfield next to his first wife. Sarah was buried in the Vert family plot in Crownland under the name Sarah Vert Jones.

Now moving forward forty-four years—in January 1911, a Noblesville deliveryman named Bert Cloud was digging around an old shed on his property on Fifth Street, adjacent to Riverside Cemetery. Suddenly, he began to turn up human bones. Since he was north of the cemetery property line, it shouldn't have been a misplaced burial. He called some neighbors to witness and continued to dig. A few feet down, he struck a metal trunk. After clearing some space around the trunk, he broke the lock with his shovel, opened it and found a corpse covered in lime that had decayed to a partial skeleton.

At this point, he contacted the authorities, and the coroner took over the case. There were clues at first, and then some elderly residents began remembering the Woodmansee incident. This would have been meaningless, except an ornately carved signet ring was discovered on the skeleton. Using this single clue, the coroner tried to contact the Woodmansee family in Illinois. However, there were no living relatives who remembered Eugene. Finally, after more searching, they found the widow of his brother near Cincinnati, Ohio. They sent her the ring, which she recognized immediately, saying both brothers had one.

The leading theory about his death was that he had stopped at a notorious roadhouse that had been at that site and had been murdered for his money. However, the sister-in-law said that the family had gotten a message from him about trouble with the wedding and a possible rival. Until the ring proved his identity, the minister thought that Woodmansee had simply skipped out in revenge for the first refusal Sarah had made. In the end, the crime was unresolved.

The story went viral when many different newspapers picked it up. Ironically, the Noblesville newspapers for 1867 and 1911 have all been lost. However, the *Indianapolis Star* did a full-page story with illustrations, and papers around the country soon followed. The *Indianapolis News* and *Urbana Daily Courier* stories are useful for research since they were able to interview people directly connected to the event. However, the other papers just cut it down to a few paragraphs and an eye-catching headline. They would occasionally mangle the information to throw more emphasis on the romance, gore and mystery of the story—a winning combination.

Throughout 1911, one can see the story spread geographically in papers from across the nation—from Fort Wayne, Indiana; to Sheboygan, Wisconsin; to Troy, New York; to Crittenden, Kentucky; to New London, Connecticut; to the *Washington Post*; to the *San Francisco Call*; and even showing up in the *Pittsburgh Press* as late as 1914. These are just the known papers to have carried it. There were probably more.

So, while the case will probably never be solved, Woodmansee's posthumous fame spread far beyond the bounds of where he lived. Thanks to human interest, we can even study it today.[212]

Notes

Part I

1. James R. Jones III and Amy L. Johnson, *Early Peoples of Indiana* (Indianapolis: Indiana Department of Natural Resources—Division of Historic Preservation and Archaeology, 2016); Kevin C. Nolan, "Distribution Analysis of Archaeological Remains in the Upper White River Basin," *Indiana Archeology* 9, no. 1 (2014): 209–29; Beth K. McCord. "Archeological Investigations at the Hobbs' Knob and Taylor Ten Sites," *Indiana Archeology* 5, no. 1 (2010): 70–92.
2. William Clark, *Journal of Gen. Charles Scott's Journey, Ohio River to Louisville, May 1791*, Missouri Historical Society collection, mohistory.org/collections/item/A0289-01266.
3. Ryland T. Brown, *Geological and Topographical Survey of Hamilton and Madison Counties* (Indianapolis, IN: State Geologist's Report, 1884), 21.
4. John B. Dillon, *A History of Indiana, from Its Earliest Exploration by Europeans to the Close of the Territorial Government, in 1816; Comprehending a History of the Discovery, Settlement, and Civil and Military Affairs of the Territory of the U.S. Northwest of the River Ohio, and a General View of the Progress of Public Affairs in Indiana, from 1816 to 1856* (Indianapolis, IN: Bingham and Doughty, 1859), 524–25; Logan Esarey, ed., *Messages and Letters of William Henry Harrison*, vol. 2 (Indianapolis: Indiana Historical Commission, 1922), 282–83.
5. Ibid., 525–26.
6. Treaty of St. Mary's, Indiana State Library collection, blog.library.in.gov/treaty-of-st-marys.

7. *Mapping Indiana* (Indianapolis: Indiana Historical Society Press, 2015), 80–81.
8. T.B. Helm, ed., *History of Hamilton County* (Chicago: Kingman Brothers, 1880), 34; A.F. Shirts, *Noblesville Independent*, March 11, 1887, 1; letter from John G. Finch, December 18, 1893, Hamilton East Public Library vertical file; article about Fabius M. Finch, *Indianapolis News*, March 19, 1896, 5; letter by A.F. Shirts, *Indianapolis News*, April 2, 1896, 8; John G. Finch, *Indianapolis Journal*, December 18, 1898, 17.
9. Shirts, *History of the Formation*, 38.
10. Fletcher, *Diary of Calvin Fletcher*, vol. 1, *1817–1838*, 88.
11. Howard Johnson, *A Home in the Woods: Oliver Johnson's Reminiscences of Early Marion County* (Indianapolis: Indiana Historical Society, 1951), 197–98.
12. David J. Bodenhamer and Robert G. Barrows, eds., *Encyclopedia of Indianapolis* (Bloomington: Indiana University Press, 1994), 1289; Russell E. Mumford, *Mammals of Indiana* (Bloomington: Indiana University Press, 1982), 266.
13. Eugene Kinkead, *Squirrel Book* (New York: E.P. Dutton, 1980), 42–43.
14. Michael A. Steele and John L. Koprowski, *North American Tree Squirrels* (Washington, D.C.: Smithsonian Institution Press, 2001), 137–38.
15. James H. Smart, ed., *The Indiana Schools and the Men Who Have Worked in Them* (Indianapolis, IN: State Board of Education, 1876); Richard E. Banta, "Indiana's Amateur Historians," *Indiana Magazine of History* 44, no. 3 (September 1948).
16. Warren, *Reminiscences of the Long Ago*, 7.
17. Shirts, *History of the Formation*, 117.
18. Ibid., 127.
19. Fletcher, *Diary of Calvin Fletcher*, vol. 1, 105.
20. Shirts, *History of the Formation*, 283–84.
21. *Advocate* [Tipton, Indiana], April 15, 1881, 2.
22. *A Man with a Price on His Head: The Life and Times of George Boxley* (Sheridan, IN: Sheridan Historical Society, 2005).
23. *Noblesville Democrat*, December 20, 1895, 1.
24. Ancestry.com, Indiana, U.S., Marriages, 1810–2001.
25. *Advocate* [Tipton, Indiana], July 25, 1895, 3.
26. Shirts, *History of the Formation*, 118–19.
27. Will Records, 1824–1920; Author: Indiana. Circuit Court (Hamilton County); Probate Place: Hamilton, Indiana.
28. Haines, *History of Hamilton County*, 165.

Part II

29. NOAA's National Weather Service website, "Historic Crests of White River," water.weather.gov/ahps2/crests.php?wfo=ind&gage=nbli3&crest_type=historic.
30. *Noblesville Ledger*, January 16, 1937; January 25, 1937.
31. Indiana Department of Natural Resources website, "Indiana Underwater: The Flood of 1913," www.in.gov/dnr/historic/files/hp-1913_flood.pdf; *Noblesville Ledger*, March 29, 1904.
32. *Noblesville Ledger*, March 29, 1904; June 4, 1875.
33. Shirts, *History of the Formation*, 271; *Noblesville Ledger*, October 1, 1923.
34. Shirts, *History of the Formation*, 82.
35. *Noblesville Ledger*, September 12, 1944.
36. Map of Hamilton Co., Indiana (Waterloo City, IN: C.A.O. McClellan and C.S. Warner, 1866).
37. *Noblesville Ledger*, May 19, 1882; March 27, 1885.
38. Ibid., September 7, 1944.
39. Shirts, *History of the Formation*, 271.
40. Ibid., 179.
41. Haines, *History of Hamilton County*, 268.
42. *Indiana State Sentinel*, March 6, 1851; *Indianapolis News*, February 8, 1908.
43. *Indiana State Sentinel*, March 13, 1851; Carah W. Harrison to Alexander Dale, May 10, 1851, Hamilton County Historical Society collection; Fletcher, *Diary of Calvin Fletcher*, vol. 4, *1848–1852*, 273.
44. Homer B. Johnson, harvester, U.S. patent 1,629,215, filed September 1, 1922, and issued May 17, 1927; *Indianapolis Journal*, July 21, 1891.
45. A.L. Lazarus, ed., *The Best of George Ade* (Bloomington: Indiana University Press, 1985), 213–14; *Indianapolis News*, July 2, 1892; July 13, 1892; *Indianapolis Journal*, July 14, 1892; *Hamilton County Ledger*, May 20, 1892; June 10, 1892.
46. Haines, *History of Hamilton County*, 166.
47. Shirts, *History of the Formation*, 161–66; Nathan Johnson, brick mold, U.S. patent 11,127, issued June 20, 1854; Helm, *History of Hamilton County*, 103.
48. *Noblesville Ledger*, April 9, 1875; June 17, 1887; July 8, 1887; February 24, 1899; June 20, 1890.
49. *Hamilton County Democrat*, April 27, 1888; *Noblesville Ledger*, June 20, 1890; September 9, 1892.
50. *Noblesville Ledger*, June 28, 1898.

51. Shirts, *History of the Formation*, 161–66; Helm, *History of Hamilton County*, 103.
52. *Noblesville Ledger*, January 28, 1887; April 22, 1887; *Hamilton County Democrat*, April 22, 1887.
53. *Hamilton County Democrat*, March 20, 1903; April 24, 1903.
54. *Hamilton County Ledger*, October 14, 1904.
55. *Noblesville Through a Camera* (Noblesville, IN: Commercial Club, 1896).
56. *Hamilton County Ledger*, August 23, 1889.
57. *Indianapolis News*, June 14, 1898; *Indianapolis Journal*, December 26, 1890; *Monroeville [IN] Breeze*, April 9, 1891.
58. *Hamilton County Ledger*, February 10, 1893; November 10, 1893; December 8, 1893.
59. *Indianapolis Journal*, May 31, 1896; *Indianapolis News*, June 1, 1895.
60. *Logansport Pharos-Tribune*, June 3, 1896; *Fort Wayne News*, June 4, 1896.
61. *Indianapolis News*, June 22, 1896.
62. Ibid., September 15, 1896; *Fort Wayne News*, October 19, 1896.
63. Alice Armstrong, sash-fastener, U.S. patent no. 464,413, filed December 1, 1891.
64. Thomas R. Cook, machine gun, U.S. patent no. 458,268, filed August 25, 1891; *Indianapolis News*, September 19, 1891.
65. *Times-Democrat* (New Orleans), August 19, 1889, 4.
66. Thomas R. Cook, machine gun, U.S. patent no. 560,842, filed May 26, 1896.
67. John and George McDonald, Tellurian, U.S. patent no. 580,328, filed April 6, 1897.
68. W.H. and S.B. Castor, gas pressure pump, U.S. patent mo. 406, 261, filed July 2, 1889.
69. W.H. and S.B. Castor, apparatus for using natural gas for raising water, U.S. patent no. 441,056, filed November 18, 1890.
70. R. Walter Wilson, accumulator, U.S. patent no. 803,303, filed October 31, 1905.
71. *Technical World Magazine*, "Wind-Made Electricity," March 1906, 98.
72. *Our Day*, "Electricity Produced by Windmills," December 1905, 28.
73. *Scientific American*, "Domestic Electric Light Plant Driven by a Windmill," June 1, 1907, 448.
74. *Indianapolis News*, June 4, 1906, 16.
75. *Noblesville Enterprise*, June 25, 1909, 3.
76. *Hamilton County Ledger*, June 13, 1902, 1.
77. *Noblesville Enterprise*, December 3, 1909, 3.

Part III

78. Haines, *History of Hamilton County*, 193, 320; Helms, *History of Hamilton County*, 132; *Noblesville Ledger*, January 24, 1919.
79. *Hamilton County Democrat*, August 16, 1889; *Hamilton County Ledger*, August 18, 1905.
80. *Noblesville Ledger*, December 5, 1945.
81. N.D. Levinson obituary, *Hamilton County Ledger*, June 20, 1899.
82. *Noblesville Ledger*, June 29, 1899.
83. Ibid., September 27, 1878; *Republican-Ledger*, September 28, 1883.
84. Stoner, *S.O. Levinson and the Pact of Paris*, 2–3.
85. *Noblesville Enterprise*, June 12, 1908; *Noblesville Ledger*, September 23, 1915.
86. *Noblesville Ledger*, June 7, 1916; December 18, 1923; May 1, 1926; November 23, 1938.
87. *Time*, "Mr. Levinson's Way," October 13, 1930, 15.
88. *Hamilton County Democrat*, February 13, 1891.
89. *Indianapolis Star*, January 17, 1968.
90. *Los Angeles Herald Examiner*, quoted in *Noblesville Ledger*, October 20, 1962; *Noblesville Ledger*, November 9, 1962.
91. *Hamilton County Democrat*, August 1, 1884; *Noblesville Ledger*, November 14, 1884; *Hamilton County Democrat*, March 15, 1889.
92. *Noblesville Ledger*, July 8, 1887.
93. Ibid., January 24, 1890.
94. *Hamilton County Ledger*, November 13, 1891; January 20, 1893; *Hamilton County Democrat*, July 8, 1892; September 7, 1894; November 8, 1895; July 9, 1897.
95. *Indianapolis Journal*, October 30, 1896; *Hamilton County Ledger*, October 25, 1898; November 9, 1900.
96. *Hamilton County Democrat*, November 25, 1898; January 27, 1899.
97. Ibid., April 28, 1899; May 19, 1899; *Hamilton County Ledger*, July 10, 1900.
98. *Hamilton County Ledger*, "Chinese Character," July 17, 1900.
99. *Arcadian*, reprinted in the *Hamilton County Ledger*, August 21, 1900.
100. *Hamilton County Ledger*, September 13, 1901; January 13, 1903.
101. *Hamilton County Democrat*, January 30, 1903; *Hamilton County Ledger*, January 15, 1904; Ancestery.com, Indiana Marriages, 1810–2001.
102. *Indianapolis Star*, January 21, 1904; *Hamilton County Ledger*, January 22, 1904; March 25, 1904.
103. *Northern Alabama, Historical and Biographical* (Birmingham, AL: Smith and DeLand, 1888), 318; General Index to Estates, 1820–1929; Will Records,

1821–1929; Estates 1917–1920; Estate Records, 1823–1824 and 1920–1930, Author: Alabama, Probate Court (Lauderdale County), Probate Place: Lauderdale, Alabama.

104. *Indianapolis News*, April 29, 1911; *The Republic* (Columbus, Indiana), May 23, 1911.

105. *Indianapolis Star*, March 14, 1906; *Times* (Munster, Indiana), May 2, 1911.

106. *Indianapolis Star*, April 18, 1864.

107. Ancestry.com, Indiana, U.S., Marriages, 1810–2001; Indiana Archives and Records Administration, Indianapolis, Death Certificates, Year: 1911, Roll: 04.

108. *Daily Reporter* (Greenfield, Indiana), May 4, 1911.

109. *Noblesville Ledger*, April 15, 1915.

110. *Noblesville Independent*, August 11, 1882.

111. *Noblesville Ledger*, August 29, 1938.

112. *Hamilton County Democrat*, July 19, 1895; *Noblesville Ledger*, December 2, 1902; February 15, 1924.

113. *Noblesville Ledger*, April 21, 1952.

114. Historical Data Systems, comp. U.S., Civil War Soldier Records and Profiles, 1861–1865; National Archives at Washington, D.C., Compiled Service Records of Volunteer Union Soldiers Who Served with the United States Colored Troops: Infantry Organizations, 8th through 13th, including the 11th (new), Microfilm Serial: M1821, Microfilm Roll: ; National Archives at Washington, D.C., NAI Title: U.S., Civil War Pension Index: General Index to Pension Files, 1861–1934, NAI Number: T288, Record Group Title: Records of the Department of Veterans Affairs, 1773-2007, Record Group Number: 15, Series Title: U.S., Civil War Pension Index: General Index to Pension Files, 1861–1934, Series Number: T288, Roll: 219.

115. *Indianapolis News*, September 27, 1871; *South Carolina Historical Magazine*, 2001, 157, 165.

116. Stephen A. Vincent, *Southern Seed, Northern Soil: African American Farm Communities in the Midwest, 1765–1900* (Bloomington: Indiana University Press, 1999), 130–31; *Noblesville Ledger*, March 31, 1880; September 3, 1880.

117. *Noblesville Ledger*, April 9, 1880.

118. *Hamilton County Democrat*, May 23, 1884.

119. U.S. Civil War Soldier Records and Profiles, 1861–1865, Ancestry.com; *Logansport Pharos-Tribune*, August 15, 1896, 2; Ancestry.com, Hamilton County, Indiana, U.S., Compiled Records from Hamilton East Public Library, 1891–1962.

120. Ancestry.com, Indiana, U.S., Marriages, 1810–2001.

121. Ancestry.com, U.S. Army, Register of Enlistments, 1798–1914; Hamilton County, Indiana, Index to Supplemental Record Marriage Transcript 1, W.P.A. Original Record Located County Clerk's Office, Book: C-2, Page 7.
122. Ancestry.com. U.S. Army, Register of Enlistments, 1798–1914; *Noblesville Ledger*, September 30, 1898; February 3, 1899.
123. Ancestry.com, Indiana, U.S., Marriages, 1810–2001; *Indianapolis Recorder*, March 7, 1903; March 12, 1904; *Indianapolis Journal*, August 1, 1903.
124. Ancestry.com, U.S., National Homes for Disabled Volunteer Soldiers, 1866–1938; National Cemetery Administration, U.S., Veterans' Gravesites, ca. 1775–2019.
125. M.D. Lichliter, *History of the Junior Order United American Mechanics* (Philadelphia: J.B. Lippincott Company, 1909).
126. *Noblesville Ledger*, "70 Years Ago," November 13, 1946.
127. *Hamilton County Democrat*, January 30, 1903; *Hamilton County Ledger*, July 21, 1905.
128. *Enterprise* (Noblesville, Indiana), February 2, 1906; October 19, 1906.
129. *Noblesville Ledger*, December 11, 1913; October 16, 1914.
130. James Madison, *The Ku Klux Klan in the Heartland* (Bloomington: Indiana University Press, 2021); Sidmel Estes to K. Hardie, October 27, 1975, Cyrus Colter file, Hamilton East Public Library.
131. *Noblesville Ledger*, March 21, 1927, 6; April 18, 1927, 1.
132. Lois Costomiris, *Rail Fences, Rolling Pins, and Rainbows*, "We Lived above the Interurban Depot When Dad Was Station Master" (Carmel, IN: Guild Press, 1994), 183; *Noblesville Ledger*, March 28, 1929.
133. *Noblesville Ledger*, December 4.
134. Ibid., May 4, 1931; March 5, 1935; January 29, 1937; *Muncie Evening Press*, July 2, 1976.

Part IV

135. *Indiana State Sentinel*, March 2, 1863; September 27, 1864; *Richmond Weekly Palladium*, September 28, 1864; *Enterprise*, (Noblesville, Indiana) July 10, 1908; Haines, *History of Hamilton County*, 516–17.
136. U.S. Bureau of the Census, Census of 1850, Deed, Owen Williams to John Rhodes, November 4, 1848, Hamilton County Recorder's Office, Deed, John Rhodes to Nehemiah Baker, June 7, 1849, Hamilton County Recorder's Office, Deed, Aaron Lindley to John Rhodes, December 1, 1851, Hamilton County Recorder's Office.

137. *Portrait and Biographical Record of Madison and Hamilton Counties, Indiana: Containing Biographical Sketches of Prominent and Representative Citizens of the Counties, Together with Biographies and Portraits of All the Presidents of the United States* (Chicago: Biographical Publishing Company, 1893), 273–75.
138. U.S. Bureau of the Census, Census of 1860, 1870; Vincent, *Southern Seed, Northern Soil*, 55, 61–62, 95.
139. Deed, Elizabeth Rhodes and John Rhodes to Micajah Waldron, September 12, 1873, Hamilton County Recorder's Office; *Noblesville Ledger*, May 28, September 24, October 15, 1875.
140. *South Bend Tribune*, September 27, 1875; *Indianapolis News*, March 29, 1878.
141. *Bloomington Progress*, February 29, 1889; *Indianapolis News*, March 22, 1889; *Indiana State Sentinel*, June 24, 1891; *Chicago Daily Tribune*, October 30, 1892.
142. *Indianapolis News*, October 12, 1893; October 19, 1893; *Hamilton County Democrat*, October 20, 1893; *Hamilton County Ledger*, October 20, 1893.
143. *Hamilton County Times*, January 6, 1909; *Hamilton County Ledger*, January 8, 1909; Madison, *Klan in the Heartland*.
144. *Hamilton County Democrat*, July 28, 1882; *Republic* (Columbus, Indiana), July 28, 1882; *Republican Ledger*, August 4, 1882.
145. *Our Westfield* (Noblesville, IN: Image Builders, 1984), 48–51.
146. *Independent* (Noblesville, Indiana), August 18, 1882.
147. Ibid., November 15, 1883.
148. *Ledger*, December 5, 1890; December 12, 1890; *Hamilton County Democrat*, December 5, 1890.
149. *Indianapolis Star*, July 22, 1907; *Palladium-Item*, July 29, 1907; *Tampa Tribune* (Tampa, Florida), August 9, 1907.
150. *Indianapolis Star*, August 12, 1907.
151. Ibid., August 11, 1907; *Hamilton County Ledger*, August 13, 1907; *Hamilton County Times*, August 16, 1907; *Enterprise* (Noblesville, Indiana), August 23, 1907.
152. Noblesville Mayor Docket Books, Hamilton East Public Library, hosted on Indiana Memory Digital Collection, indianamemory.contentdm.oclc.org/digital/collection/p16066coll34.
153. *Star-Press* (Muncie, Indiana), August 18, 1907.
154. *Hamilton County Ledger*, May 1, 1908.
155. Ibid., April 17, 1908.
156. General Laws, H. 61, Chapter 169, An Act Concerning Public Offenses, Section 467 and 468, Baseball on Sunday, Laws of the State of Indiana passed at the sixty-fourth regular session of the General Assembly begun on the fifth day of January AD, 1905 (Indianapolis, IN: Wm. H. Burford, 1905), 693; *Hamilton County Ledger*, October 31, 1905.

157. *Hamilton County Ledger*, April 27, 1906; July 28, 1908; July 31, 1908; August 4, 1908.
158. *Enterprise* (Noblesville, Indiana), July 31, 1908; *Hamilton County Ledger*, July 31, 1908.
159. *Hamilton County Ledger*, August 4, 1908; *Hamilton County Times*, August 7, 1908; *Indianapolis News*, July 10, 1908.
160. General Laws, H. 594, Chapter 175, An Act to Amend Section 468 of an Act Passed…, Laws of the State of Indiana passed at the sixty-sixth regular session of the General Assembly begun on the seventh day of January AD 1909 (Indianapolis, IN: Wm. H. Burford, 1909), 436–37.

Part V

161. *Evening Star* (Washington, D.C.), September 26, 1860; *Indianapolis State Sentinel*, August 11, 1862; *Indianapolis Star*, August 11, 1862.
162. *Noblesville Register*, May 27, 1869.
163. *Noblesville Ledger*, August 9, 1878.
164. *New York Clipper*, July 24, 1880.
165. Ibid., February 19, 1881.
166. Stuart Thayer, *Annals of the American Circus: 1848–1860* (n.p.: Peanut Butter Publishing, 1992).
167. *New York Clipper*, September 23, 1871.
168. Ibid., August 26, 1882; September 23, 1882; *Hamilton County Ledger*, November 25, 1902; *Hamilton County Democrat*, November 28, 1902.
169. *Noblesville Ledger*, June 12, 1928.
170. *Hamilton County Ledger*, March 19, 1897; October 22, 1897; October 29, 1897; November 2, 1897; November 5, 1897; November 9, 1897; *Hamilton County Democrat*, October 22, 1897; October 29, 1897; November 5, 1897.
171. *Hamilton County Ledger*, February 4, 1898; July 15, 1898; August 19, 1898; September 27, 1898; November 4, 1898; November 11, 1898; November 15, 1898; November 18, 1898; November 25, 1898.
172. *Ledger*, December 24, 1901; April 7, 1903; August 21, 1908; September 18, 1908; *Hamilton County Democrat*, April 3, 1903.
173. *Ledger*, August 21, 1908; September 18, 1908; *Enterprise* (Noblesville, Indiana), September 11, 1908; September 18, 1908; *Hamilton County Times*, September 18, 1908.
174. *Indianapolis News*, November 23, 1901.

175. Ibid., December 19, 1901.
176. *Noblesville Ledger*, November 22, 1901.
177. Ibid., December 20, 1901.
178. Quoted in *Noblesville Ledger*, December 20, 1901.
179. *Indianapolis News*, December 19, 1901.
180. *Noblesville Ledger*, December 24, 1901.
181. *Noblesville Democrat*, December 27, 1901.
182. *Noblesville Ledger*, January 18, 1919.
183. *Sheridan News*, August 15, 1919; *Jersey Bulletin and Dairy World*, December 3, 1919.
184. *Sheridan News*, October 17, 1919; *Noblesville Ledger*, November 4, 1919.
185. *Noblesville Ledger*, December 18, 1920; July 14, 1923.
186. *Indianapolis News*, August 25, 1920.
187. *Noblesville Ledger*, December 31, 1930.
188. Ibid., June 18, 1956.
189. Ibid., June 27, 1956.
190. Ibid., July 3, 1956.
191. Ibid., August 9, 1956; August 16, 1956; August 29, 1956.
192. Ibid., August 28, 1956; Tom Rice, *White Robes, Silver Screens* (Bloomington: Indiana University Press, 2015).
193. *Noblesville Ledger*, September 4, 1956.

Part VI

194. *Hamilton County Democrat*, February 6, 1891; March 27, 1891; June 2, 1893; August 25, 1893.
195. *Hamilton County Ledger*, August 8, 1890; October 7, 1892.
196. Ibid., April 23, 1897; April 30, 1897; May 25, 1897; May 28, 1897.
197. *Enterprise*, August 20, 1909, 5; August 27, 1909.
198. *Portrait and Biographical Record*, 638–39; Edith V. Cascadden, *History of Lapel and Fishersburg (Indiana)* (Lapel, IN: Edith V. Cascadden, 1938), 169–70.
199. *Noblesville Ledger*, January 3, 1879.
200. E. Duis, *The Good Old Times in McLean County, Illinois* (Bloomington, IL: Leader Publishing and Printing, 1874), 638; *Noblesville Ledger*, January 3, 1879; Helm, *History of Hamilton County*, 131; *Hamilton County Democrat*, June 11, 1893; Shirts, *History of the Formation*, 128–29.
201. *Bloomington [IN] Post*, June 30, 1837; *Detroit Free Press*, July 25, 1837; *Bangor [ME] Daily Whig and Courier*, August 11,1837; *New Bern [NC]*

Sentinel, August 26, 1837; *Buffalo Commercial Advertiser*, September 3, 1838; *Adams Sentinel* (Gettysburg, Pennsylvania), September 10, 1838; *Maumee City [OH] Express*, September 15, 1838; *Long-Island Star* (Brooklyn, New York), September 27, 1838.

202. *Morning Post* (London, England), January 4, 1838; *Essex County Standard* (Colchester, Essex, England), January 12, 1838; *North Wales Chronicle*, January 23, 1839.

203. Ancestry.com, U.S. and International Marriage Records, 1560–1900.

204. *Noblesville Ledger*, June 1, 1877, 1.

205. Helm, *History of Hamilton County*, 93–94; *Noblesville Ledger*, July 9, July 16, August 13, August 20, August 27, 1875.

206. *The Inter-Ocean* (Chicago), June 1, 1877, 4.

207. *Indianapolis News*, July 17, 1885; July 20, 1885.

208. *Hamilton County Ledger*, April 3, 1891; *Hamilton County Democrat*, April 10, 1891; *Indiana State Sentinel*, April 15, 1891.

209. Shirts, *History of the Formation*, 220.

210. Ancestry.com, Indiana, U.S., Select Marriages Index, 1748–1993.

211. Reprinted in the *Charlotte [NC] Daily Observer*, December 15, 1904.

212. *Indianapolis News*, January 12, 1911, 1; *Indianapolis Sunday Star*, May 21, 1911; *Urbana Daily Courier*, January 14, January 19, March 20, 1911.

Selected Bibliography

Fletcher, Calvin. *The Diary of Calvin Fletcher*. Indianapolis: Indiana Historical Society Press, 1972.

Haines, John F. *History of Hamilton County, Indiana: Her People, Industries and Institutions*. Indianapolis, IN: B.F. Bowen and Company, 1915.

Helm, Thomas B. *History of Hamilton County, Indiana, with Illustrations and Biographical Sketches of Some of Its Prominent Men and Pioneers, to Which Are Appended Maps of Its Several Townships*. Chicago: Kingman Brothers, 1880.

Madison, James. *The Ku Klux Klan in the Heartland*. Bloomington: Indiana University Press, 2020.

Portrait and Biographical Record of Madison and Hamilton Counties, Indiana: Containing Biographical Sketches of Prominent and Representative Citizens of the Counties, Together with Biographies and Portraits of All the Presidents of the United States. Chicago: Biographical Publishing Company, 1893.

Shirts, Augustus Finch. *A History of the Formation, Settlement and Development of Hamilton County, Indiana: From the Year 1818 to the Close of the Civil War*. Noblesville, IN: Augustus Finch Shirts, 1901.

Stoner, John E. *S.O. Levinson and the Pact of Paris*. Chicago: University of Chicago Press, 1943.

Warren, Zina. *Reminiscences of the Long Ago: Being a Historical Sketch of the Early Settlement of Bethlehem, Now Carmel and Vicinity: With an Account of the Indians and of the Doings and Makeshifts of the Early Pioneers Who Have Passed Away with a Partial List of Their Names and a List of the Dead of Bethlehem-Carmel: An Account of Merchandising and Other Branches of Business, Accidents, Suicides, Shootings, Fires, etc. up to 1911*. Carmel, IN: Zina Warren, 1911.

About the Author

David Heighway is the Hamilton County historian. He is a native Hoosier and received his undergraduate degree in history from Western Kentucky University and his master's in history from Utah State University. He has worked at museums around the United States, including places such as Utah and Pennsylvania, as well as museums in Indiana, such as Conner Prairie. He is presently an employee of the Hamilton East Public Library, sits on the Noblesville Historic Preservation Commission and is on the board of directors of the Hamilton County Historical Society.